The Complete GCSE Drama Course

Mike Gould

Drama Permissions

A View from the Bridge by Arthur Miller, published by Random House. Extracts reprinted by permission of Random House.

An Inspector Calls by J B Priestley, published by Penguin. Extracts reprinted by permission of The Peters Fraser and Dunlop Group Limited.

Bruises by Judy Upton, published by Methuen Publishing Limited. Extracts reprinted by permission of Methuen Publishing Limited.

Dealer's Choice by Patrick Marber, published by Methuen Publishing Limited. Extracts reprinted by permission of Methuen Publishing Limited.

Fairytaleheart by Philip Ridley, published by Faber and Faber Limited. Extracts reprinted by permission of The Rod Hall Agency Limited.

Listen to Me by Kishwar Naheed, translated by Mahamood Jamal from *The Penguin Book of Modern Urdu Poetry*. Extracts reprinted by permission of Mahamood Jamal.

Maria Marten, or the Murder in the Red Barn, published by Heinemann Educational Books Limited. Extracts reprinted by permission of Bodley Head.

Mountain Language by Harold Pinter, published by Faber and Faber Limited. Extracts reprinted by permission of Faber and Faber Limited.

My Mother Said I Never Should by Charlotte Keatley, published by Methuen Publishing Limited. Extracts reprinted by permission of Methuen Publishing Limited.

Nothing Gold Can Stay by Robert Frost from *Poetry – Past and Present*, published by Harcourt Brace. Extracts reprinted by permission of Henry Holt & Company.

Oedipus the King, Sophocles, translated by David Grene from *Complete Greek Tragedies*, edited by David Grene and Richmond Lattimore. Extracts reprinted by permission of The University of Chicago.

Sheer Bloody Magic edited by Carole Woddis, published by Virago Press Limited. Extracts reprinted by permission of Carole Woddis.

The Cherry Orchard by Anton Chekhov, published by Methuen Publishing Limited. Extracts reprinted by permission of Methuen Publishing Limited.

The Rover by Aphra Behn, published by Methuen Publishing Limited. Extracts reprinted by permission of Methuen Publishing Limited.

Time and the Conways by J B Priestley, published by Penguin. Extracts reprinted by permission of The Peters Fraser and Dunlop Group Limited.

Watching Brief by Mike Gould. Extracts reprinted by permission of Mike Gould.

Photographic Permissions

With thanks to the Performing Arts Library for permission to reproduce the following, except where otherwise stated:

Cover image: *The Oedipus Trilogy* © Henrietta Butler; title page: *The Bacchae* © Clive Barda; p52: *The Bacchae* © Clive Barda, *The Oedipus Trilogy* © Henrietta Butler; p58: *Dealer's Choice* © Henrietta Butler; p66: *The Cherry Orchard* © Ben Christopher; p72: *Hamlet* © Pete Jones, *Romeo and Juliet* © Ben Christopher; p74: Pam St Clement (with thanks to Saraband Associates); p75: Judi Dench © Clive Barda; p100: *The Oedipus Trilogy* © Henrietta Butler; p101: *The Masked Ball* © Clive Barda; p140: *Oedipus Rex* © Clive Barda.

To the student

The Complete GCSE Drama Course is designed to help you find your way through the skills, ideas and techniques needed to gain a good grade and, equally importantly, gain real satisfaction and enjoyment from your course.

The book can be used in a number of ways:

- *as a full course which you follow with the guidance of your teacher*
- *as a 'dip-in' manual which helps you work on key aspects of drama*
- *as a reference for you to read and make notes from.*

There are ten chapters covering everything from basic questions about what GCSE Drama is, through to detailed performance and text work. Each of these chapters tells you at the beginning what you will cover, and then takes you through the skills or knowledge in careful, planned stages.

The 'Commentary' section is vital: it provides you with the chance to develop a skill which has often been cited by examiners as poorly done – that is, commenting and writing about your own work and the work of others. It gives real advice and practice, both for exam writing (if you have a written exam) and for verbal commentary in class or the Drama studio.

The scripts are wide and varied, and cover classic texts from writers such as Shakespeare and the first real professional woman playwright, Aphra Behn, to modern writers such as Patrick Marber and Judy Upton.

The book ends with a full-length script, Watching Brief, written by the author, and performed successfully by GCSE students, as well as a series of six assignments designed for individual or group study and work. In addition, there is a Glossary of drama terms for your reference, so that you can make sure your technical knowledge about the language of drama matches your performance ability.

Enjoy your drama course!

Contents

1 What is Drama?

1 2 3 4 5 6 7 8 9 10

This chapter will explore what the term 'drama' means to you:

- *as a GCSE subject*
- *as a wider term.*

Here are three images. Look at each one carefully.

1

2

3

Defining drama

1 In pairs or groups, see if you can match any of the words below to the pictures. List the words under the numbers 1, 2 and 3, as appropriate. Note that some words may fit more than one picture.

commercial	ritual	play	tickets
disguise	make-believe	stage	character
story	audience	acting	rehearsed

Compare your lists with a partner's. Are your words in the same columns? If not, explain your choices. Then, still in pairs, discuss which of the words – if any – best fit **your** idea of 'drama'.

Commentary

Write a first definition of what drama is. Start:

Drama is when...

The forms of drama

Drama, as a performed 'live' art form, appears in many guises. The following could all be classified as forms of drama.

Amateur theatre
local amateur dramatics
nativity plays
local amateur light opera
local dance schools and productions

Commercial theatre
stand-up comics
recordings of television plays, soaps, comedies or dramas
Christmas pantomimes
commercial opera, for example, the Royal Opera
West End plays, for example, *Cats* and *Les Miserables*

Classical theatre
touring productions of plays
Royal Shakespeare Company at Stratford
The National Theatre, London

Recreational arts
festivals such as Divali
theatre-in-education (plays with an educational message often aimed at children or teenagers)
out-of-school drama clubs
in-school drama clubs
the school play or musical
6th form or college productions

Fringe theatre
arts festivals such as the Edinburgh Festival
street theatre, including mime and one-person shows

Physical theatre
ballet companies such as Northern Ballet
Punch and Judy shows

In a small group, discuss which of these you have seen, listened to or been involved with, or any drama forms not listed here.

Commentary

Write about the production or drama experience that you remember best, for either good or bad reasons.

- Start with how old you were and whether it was your first experience of 'drama/theatre'.
- Then say what was so memorable – the production, the experience of going, the excitement, the boredom, how good it was, how bad it was…
- Conclude by mentioning your most recent experience (if it was different) and whether that was worse or better.

The word 'drama'

The word 'drama' appears regularly in our everyday lives – in conversations, on television, in what we hear on the radio, in what we read in newspapers:

> "... and there was drama today when the Prime Minister suddenly sacked the Chancellor after..."
>
> "... a dramatic rescue took place at sea this evening during the worst storms for fifty years... "
>
> "Don't make such a drama out of it. I'll buy you another one tomorrow."
>
> "And United's chances of promotion were dramatically reduced by losing to City by three goals to nil."

In each of these cases, the word 'drama' – or its linked words – is used to convey a sense of excitement, of heightened experience (like the picture which comes to mind of the United team sitting in the dressing room being shouted at by an irate manager), of something larger than normal life, and different from it. There would be no 'drama' if United had simply drawn the game.

So, drama can grow out of the ordinary **into** something extraordinary. And for drama to happen in real life, we need to see life on a 'normal', or straight path, and then see an event, a moment cut across it.

Now try the following task:

1 As a class, form a line to the side of the drama room, leaving reasonable space between each student. Taking it in turns, one person at a time walks along the line. As he or she passes each member of the class, that person calls out an event to which the person walking must respond in words and actions.

The four elements of drama

So, drama exists in real life, and also as something that is created and performed for others *from* life. If real-life drama shares things in common, so does performed drama. Look again at the pictures on page 6. They all share the following:

- A *setting* or a performance *space* (even the children dressing up have this, albeit an imaginary one).
- A *relationship* between performer and audience (what we might call the 'dynamic'). The children are both performers and the audience, enjoying their own 'play', in the same way as the villagers make up both cast and viewers.
- A sense of 'otherness', of disguise, of becoming someone or something else, whether it's a character, an ancestor or an adult. In other words, being a *representation*.
- A *story* or narrative, something being told: the children dressing up as grown-ups and going shopping, the villagers recreating the story of the seasons, the actors singing a story of love, revenge, dreams…

It is well worth considering these four elements whether you are performing, watching or directing. The diagram below is a useful way to remember them.

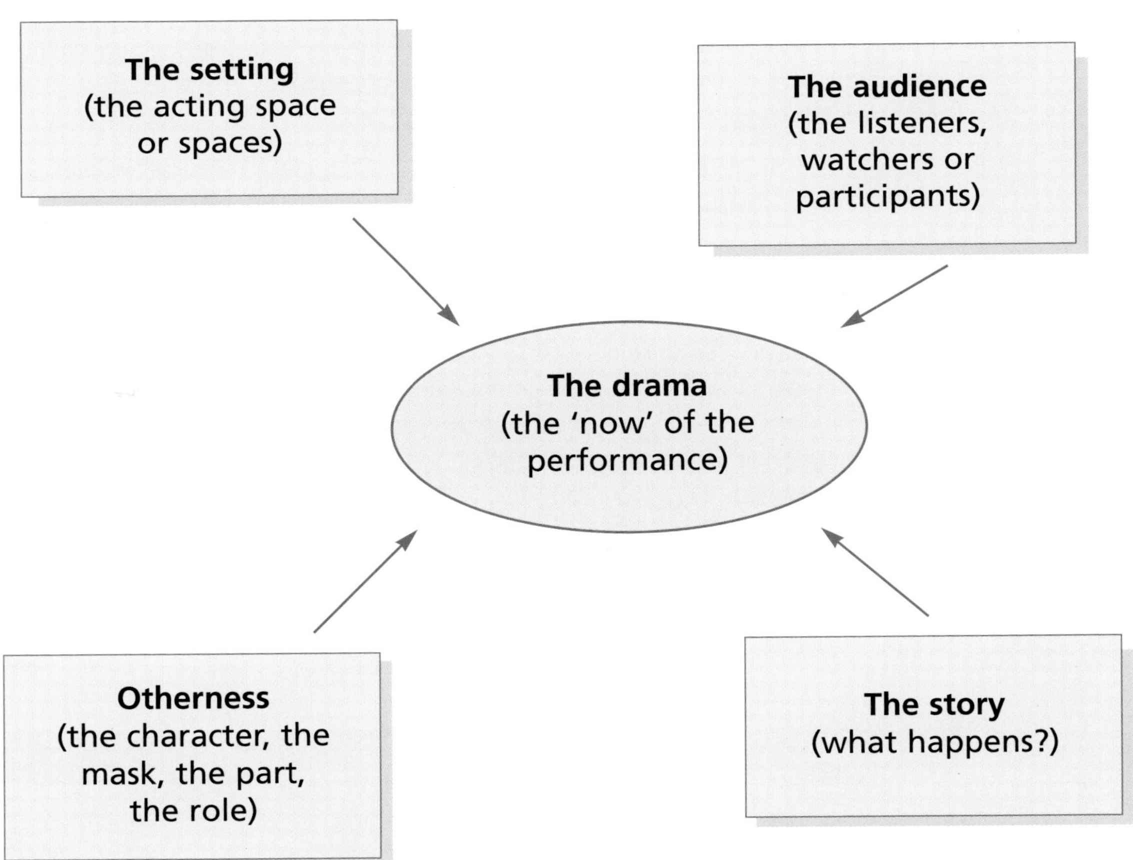

Seven exercises on drama forms

Work through each of the following exercises. As you do each one, consider to what extent the four elements we have identified are used. You might like to copy out and use this table for help.

Exercise	Setting?	Audience?	'Otherness'?	Story?
1.				
2.				
3.				
4.				
5.				
6.				
7.				

Exercises

1. Individual mime: washing the car.
2. Individual mime: arriving at your new office for the first time; being left to 'sort your things out' by your boss.
3. Whole class: sit in a circle and pass an object round (provided by your teacher, for example, a comb or a mug). Each person should pretend the object is something else when they receive it (perhaps a microphone or a hat, and so on).
4. Whole class: form a circle and develop a pose (such as the sitting position with crossed arms). Then, on the teacher's word, copy someone else's pose. Then copy a different person's pose, and so on.
5. Whole class: repeat the original pose. Then, one at a time, add a simple phrase to express a feeling or attitude, perhaps, "I'm bored" or, "It's freezing", etc.
6. In groups of four: agree a space within the drama room (it can be marked off or imaginary). Divide into the audience (two people) and the performers (two people). Perform an improvisation lasting one minute in which 'A' loses his or her winning lottery ticket, and 'B' helps to find it. Make sure there is a clear beginning and ending.
7. In groups of four: sit in your group and, in turn, tell a true story about something that has happened to you. It should last no more than three minutes.

Commentary

Write half a page on what drama is, and what the key components are. You may wish to revise and extend your earlier definition.

What is GCSE Drama?

Basically, GCSE Drama assesses or examines:
- knowledge and understanding
- skills.

Knowledge and understanding is measured by:
- the way you *talk* and/or *write* about work you have *done* or *seen*
- the way what you have learned is *demonstrated* in the *production* or *performance work* you do.

Skills are measured in similar ways, but with more emphasis on the second point above – what you demonstrate or *show* in your work.

From these two strands, there are a number of key areas that it is worth spending time on in order to perform better – both literally as a performer, and as a critic of work.

Like any other subject, drama has its own language and terminology. It is unlikely that words such as 'frozen tableau', 'mime', 'status', 'down-stage left' or 'follow-spot' will appear much in Maths lessons!

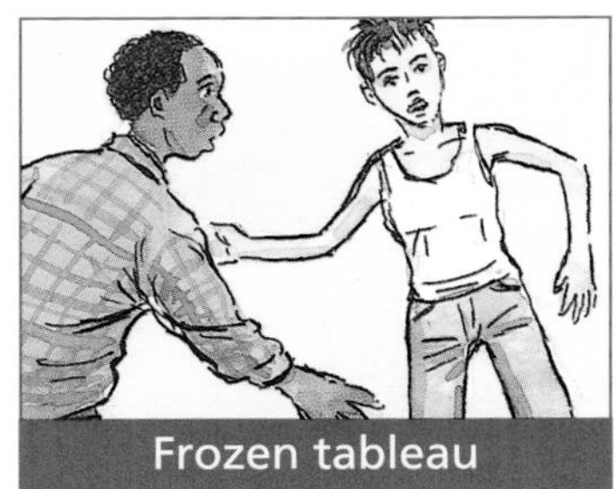
Frozen tableau

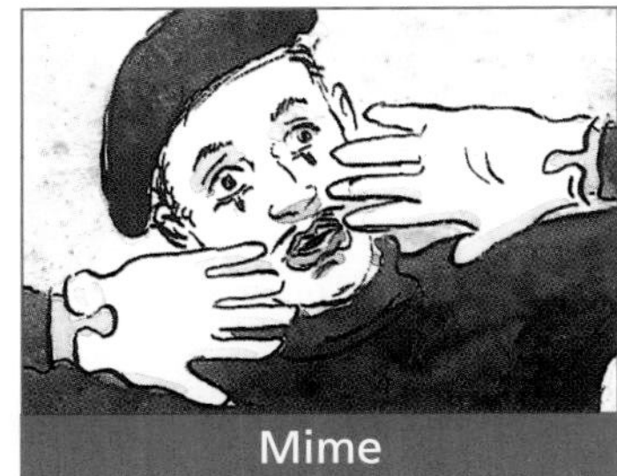
Mime

Status

Down-stage left

Follow-spot

Similarly, drama is very physical. Many professional actors train in the same way athletes do, especially if their roles require long or very active performances.

In your school, the drama department might even be linked with the PE or dance department, although it is commonly part of English – probably because of the historical link between studying written plays and performing them.

A guide to top performance

The following is a useful checklist of key points which will lead to success in your drama work on a day-to-day basis. They will be explored and developed further as the book goes on. The key words and phrases have been highlighted for you.

1 The way you work with others:

- **Contribute** to discussions, but **don't dominate**. Provide leadership, if needed, but be prepared to take a backseat on occasions, too.
- **Listen** and **encourage** others.
- **Be reliable** (turn up for rehearsals, carry out your promises).
- **Learn** lines, remember movements, bring in the right clothes, etc.
- **Be prepared to offer solutions** to any problems you highlight.

> **Key Pointer!**
> Much of your success in drama is dependent on group success. If you do well, the rest of your group, or your partner, will also do well. And vice versa.

2 How you talk and/or write about drama:

- **Learn the technical language** of drama (for example, it is important to your explanations that you know what 'down-stage left' means).
- Use a **range of appropriate phrases and words** to express your thoughts (for instance, know what phrases such as 'shaping drama' mean).
- Use **writing skills developed in English** to order your thoughts (for instance, use discourse markers such as 'however', 'in general', etc.).
- **Keep notes**, both ones that are **concise and to the point**, and others that reflect more general ideas of work-in-progress.
- **Listen to, or watch, other people** talking about drama (whether other students, critics on television or actors).

> **Key Pointer!**
> It would be great if GCSE Drama were just about your acting ability. However, finding the right words to talk or write about it isn't just helpful for your grade, it can really improve your performance work, too.

3 **Know the syllabus:**

- Make sure you **know the particular emphasis your syllabus places** on the various skills you are working on.
- Find out **what aspects are assessed** and which are 'just practice' (if any).
- If you have a **final exam**, or a **visit** by a moderator or examiner, **find out when it is** – it's no good being brilliant at the wrong time!

Key Pointer!
Get hold of your own copy of the syllabus if you can from your teacher or from the exam board. Make a chart of times in the year when you will be expected to produce assignments or final performance work.

You might like to copy and use the chart below:

Exam Board and subject title	
Minimum requirements (for example, two assessed performances)	
% of marks for performance	
% of marks for written coursework	
% of marks for written final exam	
% of marks for… (add your own details)	
Key dates or times of year (such as when you sit the exam, when devised performance is planned to finish, etc.)	

4 **And finally…**

Treat drama as a serious subject, worthy of debate and high-level skills. Don't downgrade it as 'only play' or a 'bit of fun', even if it is those things as well.

Commentary

Write down which of the aspects above you think will present you with most difficulty and think of ways to tackle them.

2 The Drama Space

Stage-work

During your course, you will see many types of dramatic performance – some outdoors, some within your own drama room or school hall, some with period costume with make-up, and so on. However, for most people outside a Drama GCSE course, their idea of a 'theatre' – the place where plays take place – will be a large-ish building with a stage, with the audience sitting in front of the actors, possibly in rising rows to the back. In fact, something like this:

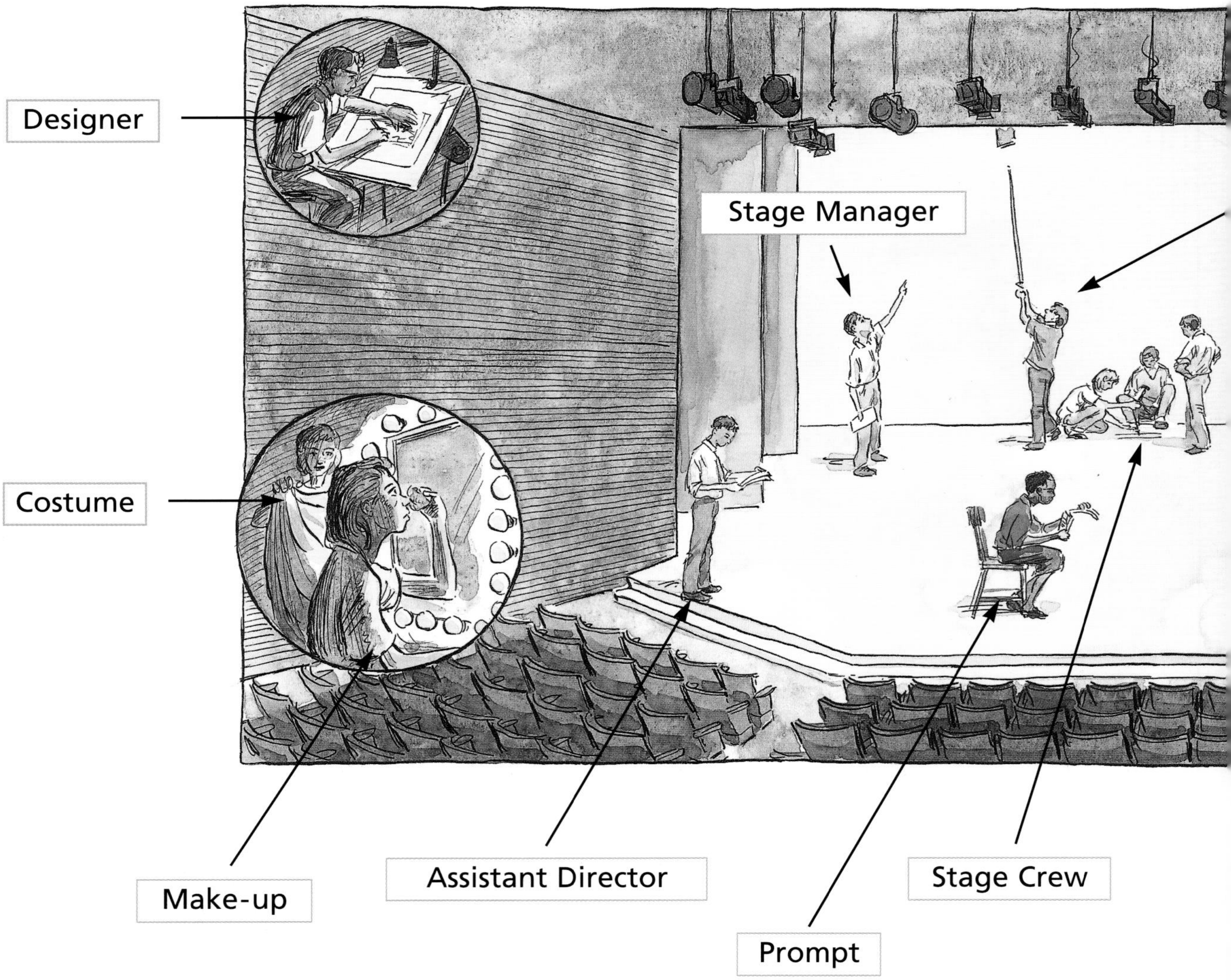

Designer
Stage Manager
Costume
Make-up
Assistant Director
Stage Crew
Prompt

Try sketching the stage and seating of your local theatre, either in the same style as this page or as an overhead plan.

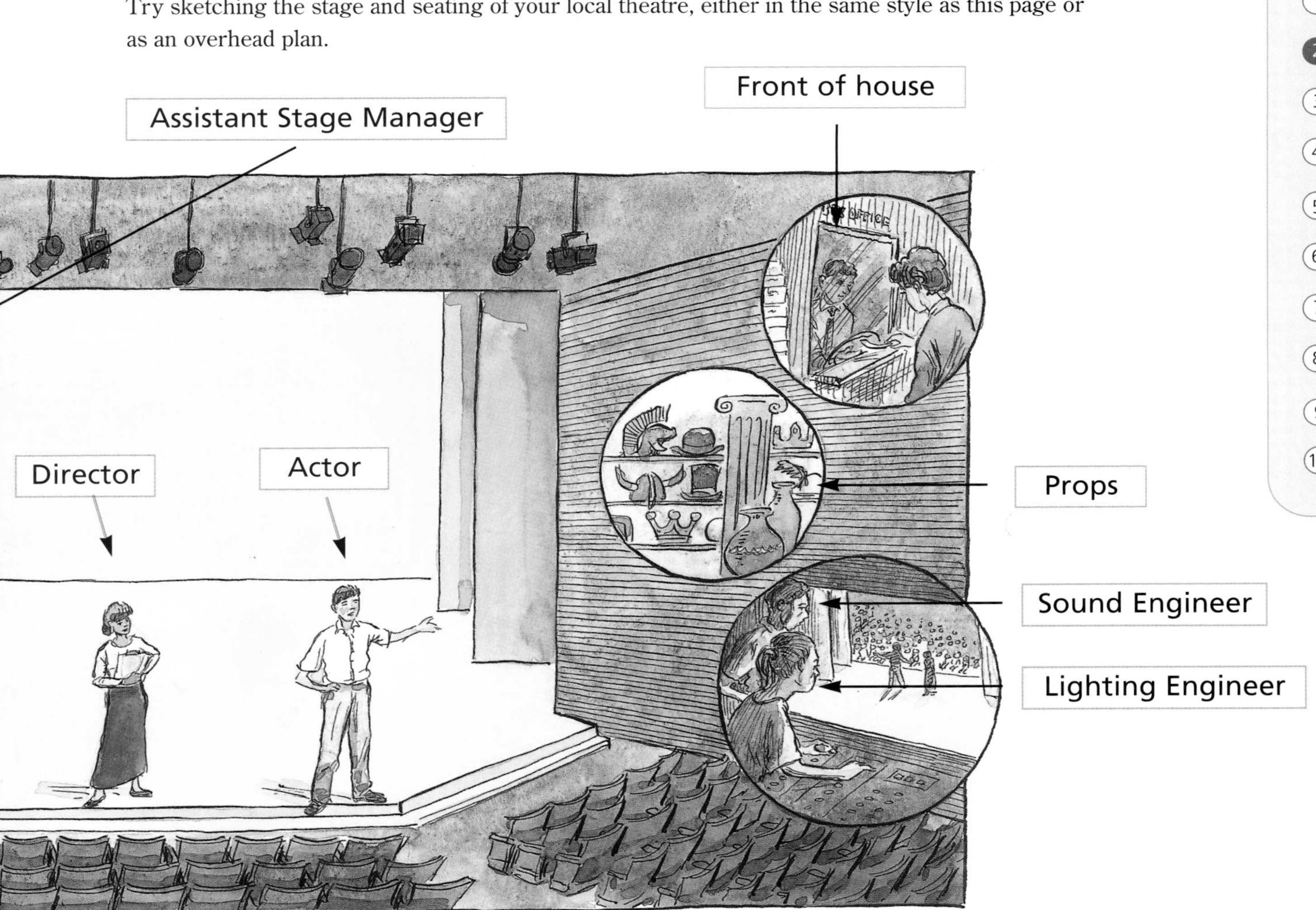

Commentary

Make some brief notes on the following:

- How close is this representation to the theatre you know best, preferably a local one?
- Have you ever been backstage, or seen where the lighting and sound is controlled?
- When you see a live performance, how aware are you of all the factors that have gone into it?
- Is there a particular aspect that interests you?

The acting space and roles

What does this recipe of people, jobs and drama space mean for your work?

First, look at the **roles** each person has. If you are in a group of four, it is clear you cannot fully cover roles with five or more characters. However, aspects of those roles are important, and you can always find ways to cover yourself.

Commentary

Consider any piece of drama you are thinking of doing. What roles are needed and how can they be split?

Another aspect to consider is the **technology**. You might not have access to a sound suite or a lighting system, but there are other, perhaps more appropriate, ways to generate noise or illumination.

1 In your group, brainstorm all the different ways you could convey the following idea called *Time running out*. Don't forget to consider musical instruments, voice, bodies, objects, materials…

2 Now perform a one-minute piece called *Time running out*. Have one person acting while the rest of you provide the sound using only your bodies and voices (but no words).

What is the acting space?

Space, and your use of it, is dealt with more specifically in Chapter 4; however, defining the whole acting space – the area used by the performers – is equally important.

1 When you see a performance somewhere, discuss in your group:
- how you know what the acting space is
- how you know where the acting space begins and ends.

2 Divide your group equally into the 'audience' and the 'performers'. The 'audience' should sit on the floor.

3 The remaining members of the group should now perform any reasonably brief drama they are working on, or have completed recently (use *Time running out*, if you wish). They must make a conscious decision WHEN and WHERE the action begins.

4 Perform for one minute, then stop.

5 The other members of the 'audience' group should now try to say when and where they thought the acting began.

Commentary

Discuss as a whole group whether the audience were right. Does it matter if they think the performers were acting when they weren't? Are there reasons why the actors might want the audience to be unsure if they were acting or not?

Making an acting space

Below are four different ways in which a simple acting space can be created in a drama studio or room using 15–25 chairs. Look at each one carefully.

'Circle' or 'in the round'

'Semi-circle'

'Rows'

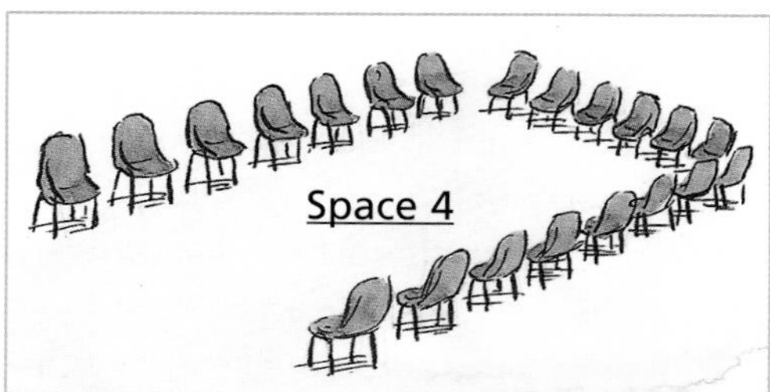

'Horseshoe' or 'thrust stage'

1 Discuss, in your groups, the advantages and disadvantages of each one of these arrangements. Consider:

- what it is like for the audience in terms of the sound, the sight-lines, closeness to the action, and so on
- what it is like for the performers with regard to their spatial awareness, their sight-lines, effect on voice and movement, etc.

You might like to copy and use this table. Look at the examples below.

Space	Advantages	Disadvantages
1	Real sense of audience involvement.	
2		
3		People at back very distant from action.
4		

2 Choose any short extract from a piece of drama you know or are working on. Try performing it in each of the four different arrangements. After each session, discuss which worked best for the actors and which for the audience.

Other spaces

There are common perceptions of how drama should be performed or presented. For example:

Acting position
Performers in front of, and often below, rows of spectators.

Acting space
Square or other four-sided stage, often slightly raised from the ground.

Audience position
Directly in front, or slightly to the side, of the stage.

Audience space
Rows of seats, often at different levels (the 'stalls', 'circle', etc.).

However, as you have already seen, it doesn't have to be like this. Nowadays there are many different ways of performing, and one example is the *promenade theatre*. This is when a performance, and the audience, move from one location to another. It often takes place in a building, but it could equally be in a series of outside locations.

1 Choose a well-known fairytale and sketch a storyboard using a series of locations within the school, or in the local area, to which an audience could go as the performers and story move on.

For example:

Actress playing Cinderella sweeps floor.

Actresses playing Ugly Sisters discuss their plans.

Commentary

Having looked at a small number of acting space possibilities, write about the one that you find most interesting. Is there any piece of drama you know which would be particularly suited to your preferred choice? What problems might there be using the acting space or spaces you prefer?

3 Voice and Sound

This chapter will:

- *explore the possibilities of using voice and sound in drama*
- *show how different approaches to voice and sound can improve a performance.*

Vocal effects

Have you ever thought about the sounds we make when we are speaking? Not just the words, but the 'ums', 'ahhs', the intake of breath, the gasp, the cry – even the movement of our bodies or our feet on the floor.

We don't often consider these things as most of our speech is made naturally and without thinking. But on the stage, we are being watched, listened to, observed.

1 Try this piece of dialogue with a friend:

A:	Jo?
B:	Yeah.
A:	What do you think about...
B:	Huh?
A:	Are you listening?
B:	Sorry. 'Course I am.
A:	No, forget it.

Does it sound 'natural'?

2 Now learn it by heart by practising it again and again, until you feel completely comfortable with the words.

You have probably made some unconscious decisions about the two people involved, A and B. You may feel A is being ignored; you might think B is bored, or feels guilty. Unknowingly you will have added to the words on the page and it is inevitable that certain vocal effects will have started to affect the way your character comes across.

These vocal effects might be:
- the speed at which you speak
- the volume – whether it is quiet or loud
- the stress you place on individual words, or parts of words
- the speed of response (how quickly one person's words follow the others)
- the phrasing – the musicality of each word or sound.

3 Take the words, "Are you listening?"
This can be said in so many ways. Some of them might sound strange, but they can be used. Look at these visual representations of the phrase and say each one as you think it is meant to be said.

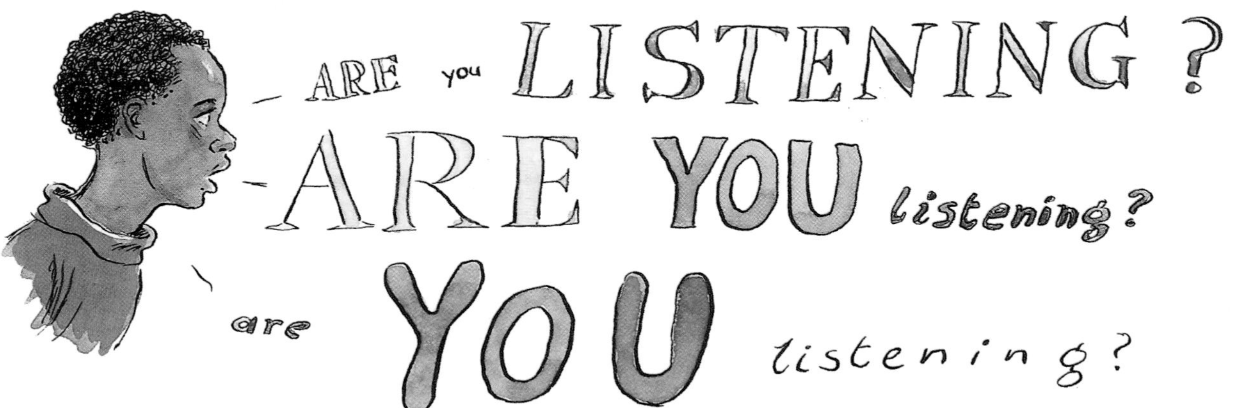

Vocal exercises

In order to break up 'ordinary' dialogue and to make it come alive and mean something, it can help to play around with it so that words start to have different emphases, or stand out suddenly.

1 Try these exercises with the A/B dialogue on page 20:
- say the dialogue with random lines, in any order you wish
- repeat the dialogue, but say it in reverse order with the last line first
- take your lines (A or Bs) for a walk around the room, saying them minus the responses.

2 Finally, stop speaking and think about your lines. Decide at least three basic things about the dialogue:
- how quickly you are going to speak
- a particular line you are going to emphasise or draw attention to
- a basic 'attitude' for your character (perhaps cross, bored, nervous, etc.).

3 Discuss each line, explaining how you intend to say it and deciding how quickly you will speak or respond, and when.

4 Now perform the dialogue.

1 2 3 4 5 6 7 8 9 10

The 'colour' of words

You have probably experienced a time when you have thought about a word so much it suddenly seems strange. If you say your own name often enough, it can start to sound weird after a while – as if you've never really heard it before.

It is sometimes said that words have their own colour, texture and shape.

1 Read this list silently to yourself, sounding the words out in your head.

stingray
porthole
conundrum
pit
harrowing
log-jam
airy
eye
feather
babbling

2 Now say each one in turn slowly, sounding out in full the vowels and syllables (without mispronouncing the word). For example, for 'pit', place your lips firmly together for the 'p', and make sure you sound the sharp 't' at the end. Concentrate on the sound, not the meaning.

Commentary

Choose five words from the list above. Describe their sound using some of the words below, as well as words of your own.

light heavy sharp soft vague
clear musical dull decent
dark bright red white black
small sensible silly simple

Now choose any speech or set of lines from a play you have read or are studying and look at the words in it. Do they have a particular colour, texture or shape? Write about what you find.

3 Now look at this collection of neologisms (made-up words):

glob	timuli	penty-pinty
missily	toberise	lillifying
spinter	mallified	tresser
scarched	bote	aculate
durgan	glamming	gorably
dool	butlefixer	mungrun
santh		pamil

Imagine they come from two speeches given by humans in the year 2050. The first is a speech by the Prime Minister describing an attack on Europe by another planet. The second is by someone describing a beautiful ballet.

4 Draw a table with the headings below and, judging by their sound, insert the words under the correct heading.

Prime Minister's speech	Ballet speech

When you have finished, select one of the speeches and improvise a performance of it to the rest of the class or to your group. (You may need to add ordinary English words to make it work.)

> For example:
>
> I have some durgan news. We have been toberised by…

(Note: you may need to change the endings of some words to make them fit the sentence, so *toberise* becomes *toberised*.)

5 Now develop this speech into a piece of drama in which the characters all speak in this way. You will need to invent some more neologisms first!

Attack and breathing

One of the keys to making each line or expression meaningful in performance is what's called 'attack'. Here are two first lines of dialogue:

1 Try saying each one aloud to a partner, as if in conversation.

You will notice that, "Tell me…" are easier words to get your mouth around and make strong than, "Whether he's…". It's easier to 'attack' the strong 'T', and it's difficult to run, "Tell me" into one word or sound. 'W' is relatively weak as a sound, and 'he' is easily mixed with the end 'r' to make 'Whether-'e's'.

2 Now try saying the first line with the emphasis on the words in capitals. Make a special effort to sound the first syllable:

WHETHER he's ALIVE or DEAD, I can't tell.

This may sound awkward, and perhaps a little unnatural, but there is little doubt it will make an impression on the audience.

3 Now try saying the line with different words emphasised (keep WHETHER strong each time).

Your own scripts

Select any sequence of dialogue, perhaps of seven or eight lines, featuring more than one character. In pairs, or as a group if there are more than two characters, play the lines, paying special attention to the opening word of each – either by clearer speech, or with louder voices.

Breathing

Breathing is an important consideration, both for professional actors and many amateur performers. For much of your work you will not be expected to project your voice long distances to the back of a large theatre, but you will have to be heard and understood by fellow students, the teacher and, perhaps, the examiner within the drama studio or room.

Clearly, some basic vocal and physical warm-ups before performing are advisable, but as a general rule:

1 Breathe from the diaphragm (pit of the stomach) and not the chest.

2 Practise all the sounds of the language in turn, so that your mouth and tongue become familiar with the special features of each. We have a habit, in normal speech, of swallowing many sounds so that words or parts of words are lost.

Here are just five possible sounds that you can practise forming. Try them in two different ways: first as short 'spat out' sounds, then as longer, drawn-out sounds.

b, b, b, b, b (as in Bob)
s, s, s, s, s
w, w, w, w, w
oo, oo, oo, oo, oo (as in moon)
k, k, k, k, k (as in kick)

The repetition of consonants in front of vowels in a sequence is also helpful. For example:

bah, bah, bah, bah, bah

bay, bay, bay, bay, bay

be, be, be, be, be, be

bau, bau, bau, bau, bau

boo, boo, boo, boo, boo

Commentary

It is not the scope of this book to give you detailed breathing or sound-forming exercises but, as a matter of interest, try to work out how many different 'mouth shapes' English requires (for example, 'w' and 'oo' are quite close in shape, 'k' is quite different).

'Attack' in longer speeches

One difficulty comes with longer speeches, especially monologues of great power or with strong images (word pictures).

The following speech has no obvious pauses for breath, except in the penultimate line, but each key line or image must be given due weight. It comes from Shakespeare's *Macbeth*. Lennox is telling Macbeth, a Scottish lord, about the terrible night's weather that has just passed. The audience also knows that Macbeth has murdered the king in his bed during the same night.

Lennox: The night has been unruly: where we lay,
Our chimneys were blown down, and, as they say,
Lamentings heard i'th'air, strange screams of death
And prophesying with accents terrible
Of dire combustion and confused events,
New hatched to th'woeful time. The obscure bird
Clamoured the livelong night. Some say, the earth
Was feverous and did shake.

1. First of all, read it in your head and see if any key words or phrases stand out naturally as strong or powerful. Reread the speech five or six times in your head until you are familiar with it.

2. This time read it aloud, but sound out each word artificially so that each consonant is clear, and none are shortened or dropped (like 'h's or 't's). It might be very slow, but try to keep going without taking too many breaths.

3. Now go through the speech and identify the key words or phrases to which you are going to give special emphasis.

4. Reread the speech aloud, making sure you 'attack' the first two words, and this time keeping up a reasonable pace, but making the words clear.

Commentary

Focusing on the sounds and the words should help you to understand and make meaning of the speech. Now write a description of your own reading where you emphasised words, and perhaps whether you were able to make the whole speech 'hang together' without taking too many breaths.

For example:

> I started with a strong attack on 'The night' because that is the key focus of the speech, but I wanted to work towards 'the earth' as a key phrase as I wanted to draw attention to the effect of the murder. Therefore, I raised my voice as if to suggest a question on 'earth' as if I couldn't quite believe it.

Sounds for meaning

Most of the previous practice assumes there are only two ways to say words – with emphasis (strong or loud) and without emphasis (weak and quiet). But think how frightening a whispered line, said with menace and emphasis, can be.

1 Say these words as if you were a kidnapper threatening someone over the phone:

> Think carefully. Think very carefully. Then send the money. That way, no one gets hurt.

2 Now try projecting your whisper across the room. Ask your partner to stand six or seven metres away, and then say one of these three lines. (Make sure they cannot see the words.) Can they hear each word clearly?

> Nobody will ever know that it was me – do you hear? Nobody!

> Take the key from the draw and place it in the wardrobe lock; turn it, and stand well back.

> All the infection that the sun sucks up on Prosper fall and make him by inchmeal a disease!

The different vocal effects or sounds in a voice tell people a great deal about a person's state of mind. Look at the following words which we use to describe one form of speech:

> cry
> shout
> moan
> groan
> sigh

When we see a line in a script, we are often not told how it is to be said. For example, take this line:

> Nobody cares!

The only clues to how to speak this line come from the actual meaning of the words, and perhaps from the exclamation mark, which suggests some 'force' in the voice.

3 Now, at random, select from the previous page one of the five ways of speaking, and say the line to a partner. He or she should then tell you which of the ways of speaking you selected. If your partner can't tell which way you chose to speak, what do you think you need to do to make it clearer – raise the pitch? Speak softly? Emphasise one word? For example, is a 'shout' gruffer and more controlled than a 'cry', which might be higher pitched?

Here's one way of interpreting the line:
Stress on 'nobody' to emphasise the character's loneliness…

Nobody cares!

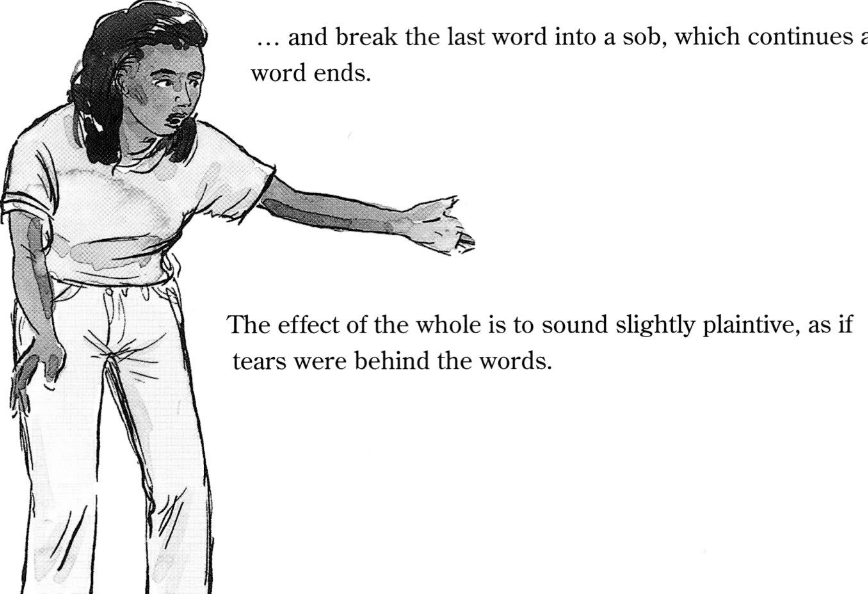

… and break the last word into a sob, which continues after the word ends.

The effect of the whole is to sound slightly plaintive, as if tears were behind the words.

Commentary

It is important to find ways to describe how you say or hear lines spoken on stage. Adjectives which describe the tone of voice (such as 'plaintive') are very useful, as are the verbs describing the manner of speaking (such as 'groan' or 'sigh'.)

Copy and complete this passage about an imaginary performance, add suitable verbs and adjectives.

> Maria's first lines on the stage are a ____________ cry of despair at the betrayal by her husband. He bumbles about the stage, ____________ that he always loved her, but her responses are ____________ and ____________ .
>
> When her son enters, he takes his mother to one side and ____________ urgently: "Leave him! He has destroyed us."

Laughter and tears

1 There are, of course, all sorts of other sounds beyond words which are easily understood. With a partner, try each of these in turn:

A sigh
A yawn
A gasp
A laugh
A cry

2 It is probable that each of these sounded quite different depending on who did it. Your partner's idea of a gasp may be more or less strong than yours. The words on the page alone aren't enough to show the full range of emotions these sounds offer. However, if we then add further detail… Try these now:

A sigh – of regret as you come across an old photo of someone with whom you have lost contact.

A yawn – of extreme boredom at a dinner party (which you are trying to conceal).

A gasp – of delight at a surprise gift.

A laugh – despising someone's foolish attempt to do something.

A cry – of despair as a set of car keys disappears down a drain.

Finally, there are all the speech sounds, both conscious and unconscious, that we add to the words we say – the umms, errs, the pursing of the lips, the 'tutting' that accompanies the shake of the head, and so on.

3 Take any speech from a text you are studying and, once familiar with it, speak it aloud to your partner. Add appropriate speech sounds, such as those above, to express hesitation, surprise, reflection, etc. Ask your partner to identify those sounds. How many were ones you'd consciously added? How many were 'natural'?

Commentary

Laughter and crying are two of the most difficult things to do convincingly when you perform. Write about why this might be, and note down any ideas for how you could make them convincing.

4 Space and Movement

This chapter will:

- *look at the way space can be used to convey meaning in performance*
- *look at the way different types of movement and gesture enhance characterisation and storytelling.*

Starting positions

It seems obvious to think about space, movement and gesture when we act, but often this is reduced to such things as:

- making sure you come onto the stage at the right time
- standing where you stood during rehearsal
- remembering to pick up a particular object or open a door
- ensuring your buttons are done up, that your hat doesn't fall off, etc.

Of course, these are important things and many productions or performances would fall apart without them. However, to a large extent it is the focus and detail that really makes an average performance into something that is 'truthful', and in which characters have impact.

The list below details some of the key aspects to address and can act as a sort of 'memory-aid' for you:

1. physical readiness – getting ready to perform
2. focus – making sure the small details are correct
3. positional sense – using space to make meaning
4. interplay
5. gestures
6. contrast
7. stillness
8. pace and tempo
9. objects and symbols
10. perspective

These are listed in no particular order, but each will be dealt with in this chapter.

Physical readiness

As an actor, you may have to look and behave as if you are a tired old man sitting on a bench by the beach in winter

when you are, in fact…

… a 15-year-old girl ready to leap around the room because you've just spent an hour sitting doing an essay in English on a mild day in May.

Getting yourself ready physically: three exercises

1 On your own

a) Curl yourself into a ball, on your haunches, with your hands tucked round your legs and as close to the ground without actually sitting on it as you can.

Now, slowly, and with control, count to ten and gently unfold your body until you are standing on your tiptoes with your hands raised high in the air (reach that point by the count 'ten').

Reverse the process. At all times you should be in full control.

b) Repeat the process, but this time do so as a burst of power, going from crouched position to an explosion leaping into the air, shouting, "YES!"
There's no need to return to the 'ball'.

Practise these moves several times until you can interchange between them from 'explosion' to 'control' reasonably effortlessly.

2 Pair work: moulding a statue

This is a well-known activity you might have done when you were younger. The benefit of it is that it makes you focus on the various parts of the body and their angles, shapes, weight and texture.

Using the theme 'triumph', mould your partner's body, as if it were clay, into a statue that represents that word. You are not allowed to speak and your partner must be 'clay'; however, if you place his or her arm in the air they should leave it there, not let it fall. You have 15 moves to mould the body.

Reverse roles when you have finished.

3 Group work: frozen tableaux

This is particularly useful as a way of exploring the themes of a text before you look at the script, but here it is being used more as a way of physically warming up and improving the interplay of your group.

Tell a story in a series of four statues. Each statue is a frozen mime involving the entire group – a photograph or tableau of that moment in time and space. Use your bodies to create not just human forms, but natural or inanimate ones (for example, trees and paths, etc.).

The four frozen statues are: **Childhood**, **Forest**, **Fear** and **Wisdom**.

Practise until you can move seamlessly from one to the other so that the whole series of statues becomes one slide show of images. Remember, there is no speaking!

Actions not words

It is possible to tell a whole drama without a single word being said. Look at this situation carefully.

- A man is at home.
- He is getting ready for an interview for a new job and is taking care to brush his hair, put on a tie, and so on.
- He moves to where he thinks the key for the car is.
- It isn't there.
- He searches – at first with some control and thought, but increasingly, as it becomes clear that the keys are mislaid, desperately as panic sets in, and the search becomes an urgent trawl of the room.
- He is unsure whether to phone or not, concerned at the impression that might be created.
- In the end, having looked everywhere, he slumps on the sofa, having given up.
- As he comes to terms with what's happened, his eye catches sight of the keys, in the one place he didn't look.
- He grabs them and races out of the door.
- Once outside he stops for a moment – he realises that a key item of clothing (tie, hat, shoes, etc.) has been left off.
- He returns to the front door and searches his pockets.
- He has left the door key in the flat.

END

1 On your own, run this piece through, conveying the change from anxious control to all-out panic. Use the symbols below as a memory aid.

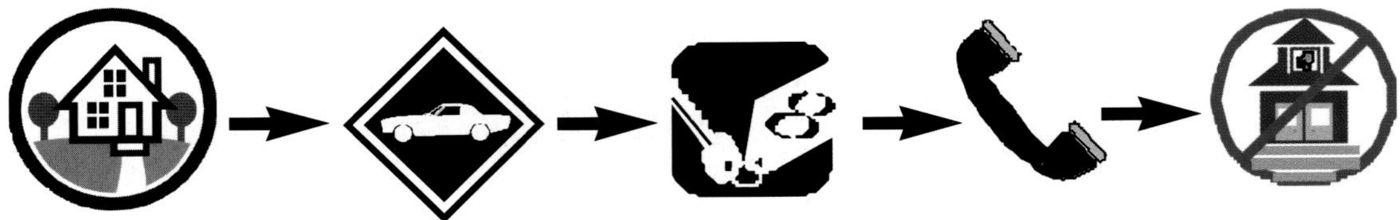

2 Now work in a group. Select one member of the group to perform the piece. At any given moment, a member of the group can stop the performance and suggest a change to a gesture, movement, position, etc. When it has been tried, the group can say whether it should be adopted in the final performance.

Focus on gesture

Focus is all-important. Look at this example of how a simple gesture can convey meaning.

Moment: The man or woman gets ready for the interview.
Gesture: With the tips of their fingers they brush hairs from their jacket whilst looking in the mirror.
Meaning: Conveys concern with appearance.

This can be developed further.

Gesture: The person moves away from the mirror, looks down at their jacket, stops before they have gone three paces, returns and brushes the same spot again.
Meaning: Conveys an over-anxious nature that can be played on later in the scene.

The range of simple everyday movements that we take for granted become all-important on the stage. Each of the following are gestures or movements we do every day:

Sitting down in a chair
Standing up again
Getting out of bed
Using a knife and fork
Drinking from a cup or glass
Opening a door
Closing a door
Walking from one spot to another

1 Apply some or all of these to any of the roles or characters below:
- a prisoner on his or her first day in prison
- a top sports star being followed for the day by a television programme
- a young man or woman arriving in a hostel for his or her first proper night's sleep.

Your own scene or work

2 Apply this sort of detail to any sequence or scene from your current work. You can stop at any moment and 'interrogate' yourself or other members of the group.
- What are you feeling?
- How can your face show this? Should your face show anything?
- What small, or grand, gestures can you add to clarify the idea of this character to the audience?

Commentary

When each person in the group has had a chance to perform and be directed, discuss which actions and gestures seemed to work best and, also, where there were problems.

Pair movement and space

Now work with this simple dialogue.

A: Hello.
B: Hello.
A: Have you been here long?
B: No, not really.
A: Is there something you'd like?
B: No, I'm fine thanks.

1 Read it in pairs a couple of times until you know it by heart.

2 Now try the dialogue using each of these basic positions (you can 'mix and match them' or stay in the same position throughout).

Commentary

Discuss briefly the five different uses of space. Did anything emerge about the characters as a result? 'Turning the back' is often a shorthand for ignoring someone or showing displeasure. Did this happen in your performances?

As an improvisational exercise, continue the pair dialogue, perhaps by selecting one of the five suggested starting positions, and then let the drama develop out of it.

Keep to a top limit of five minutes improvisation time.

Pair work and a chair

3 Now, using the same dialogue as on the previous page and using a chair, perform the piece again in the following five ways:

Commentary

Discuss the *function* of the chair in this dialogue. The use of a chair can symbolise power ('this is my chair; I'm keeping it') or weakness (B is lower in height and, therefore, might appear trapped by the chair, rather like a police suspect), or any number of other possibilities. What effect did the use of the chair have in each case?

Pair work and touch

4 Now try the dialogue again, with or without the chair, and introduce any one of the following forms of physical contact:

a. a light touch on the arm at some point in the dialogue
b. a hug
c. a kiss on the cheek.

Commentary

Discuss how the introduction of the gesture changed the relationship, or how you viewed A or B. Did it make him or her seem more intimate? More in control? Less in control?

Key moments and gestures

When performing, care should be taken that any gestures, or changes in position, are not accidental as it may have a profound effect on the way the drama is seen. Take point a), the touch on the arm. Let's imagine the dialogue was performed as if B is upset with A, who is late.

If the touch on the arm is introduced at the start, it can be rejected by B who might be making the point, "If you're looking for affection or forgiveness, think again!"

If the touch on the arm is introduced by B after A's last line, it might be seen as an act of reconciliation, or forgiveness.

The same can be true of work with the chair – or space.

4 Imagine the same situation: B is upset over A's lateness. Look at this way of playing it: notice how other gestures have been added.

A: (facing B)	Hello.
B: (remains at a distance)	Hello.
A:	Have you been here long?
B: (turns back on A)	No, not really.
A: (approaches B, stands behind)	Is there something you'd like?
B: (sits down, arms crossed)	No, I'm fine thanks.
(A rests hand lightly on B's shoulder)	
END	

Putting it all together

5 You are probably heartily sick of this dialogue by now, but try it one last time, incorporating any of the elements about space and movement you have learned from the exercises in order to make the performance have meaning and interest.

Commentary

Take any short piece of dialogue between two characters and script it in the way it has been done for A and B above. If you have time, run it through with a partner.

Or…

Use the dialogue on the next page. It is *My Mother Said I Never Should* by Charlotte Keatley.

Background to the scene

This extract is taken from *My Mother Said I Never Should* by Charlotte Keatley. It tells the story of four different women over the course of several generations, from before the Second World War to the late 1980s. The style is not 'naturalistic' – that is, there is no attempt to make the stage look as if it really is the 1920s. Also, all four actresses play themselves as babies, children, teenagers, in middle age…

However, every now and again the story pauses and the women meet in a place called 'The Wasteground'. Their language is that of small children, but what they say is a comment on what is going on elsewhere in the play.

In the 'real-time' story, Rosie is Jackie's daughter, but has been brought up by Jackie's mother. Rosie has not been told she is Jackie's daughter at this stage in the play. Obviously, in the 'Wasteground' scenes, they meet – but this should not be seen as realistic, but rather like a chorus, or comment on the main story.

Movement is important here because the actresses (who are normally 'grown women') are playing children aged, respectively, 8 (Rosie) and 9 (Jackie). Also, the scene is strongly visual with the cutting of the fingers, and the element of ritual in the chanting, skipping, and so on.

My Mother Said I Never Should by Charlotte Keatley

Scene Eight: *The Wasteground.* ***Rosie*** *skipping, chants.*

Rosie: Georgie, Porgie pudding and pie,
Kiss the girls and make them cry,
When the girls come out to play –

Jackie (*runs up, one hand behind her back.* ***Rosie*** *stops.*): I went to the boys' den.

Rosie: You said you wouldn't!

Jackie: Only slightly.

Rosie: You're out of the gang.

Jackie: I got the penknife back.

Rosie: I don't believe you.

Jackie (*takes the penknife from behind her back and holds it out between them*):
So there.

continued...

Rosie: So what?

Jackie: I kissed a boy.

Rosie: You didn't!

Jackie: I did.

Rosie: What's it like?

Jackie: I think I'm in love.

Rosie: How do you know?

Jackie: Because this boy made me cry. Daddy makes Mummy cry and she says it's because she loves him. (*Opens penknife blade*.) Now we can do the Vow.

Rosie (*backing away*): It's too late. You've probably got his seed now and it'll grow and grow and fill you up.

Jackie: You're still my best friend.

Rosie: Don't talk to me about best friends because I'm never playing with you again.

Jackie (*pause*): Kissing wasn't as good as best friends.

Rosie: Why d'you do it then?

Jackie: To get the penknife.

Rosie: You didn't need to kiss a boy. You could have given him some bubble gum.

Jackie: I did. He wanted a kiss as well. (*Pause. Jackie holds the blade up*). They said I'm a cissy.

Rosie: You are.

Jackie (*holds up index finger and ceremoniously jabs the tip with the penknife. Studies it.*): I'm bleeding.

Rosie: Do I do it too?

Jackie: Yes.

continued...

Rosie (*takes the knife and stabs her own index finger*): Ready.

They face each other and hold fingertips together and recite.

Rosie: Truth is honesty
Jackie: Honesty is true,
Keep your promise
And I'll keep you.

They step back and suck their fingers, Jackie *puts the penknife away.*

Rosie: You can't ever lie to me now. (*Pause*) Can you see into the future?

Jackie (*frightened*): A bit.

Rosie: Will you have a look for me?

Jackie (*Pause*): It'll happen anyway. Mummy says don't cross bridges.

Rosie: Is that a spell?

Jackie: I don't know. She just says it.

Rosie: At night?

Jackie: I heard her say it to Daddy, in the garage.

Pause, they look at each other.

Rosie:
Jackie: Don't cross bridges!

Rosie: It must be a spell.

Blackout.

Commentary

Having performed the piece to the rest of the group, or class, discuss and make notes on how closely you were able to convey the sense of younger children without becoming completely objects of fun – even though there is humour in the scene.

Group work and movement

Pair work allows a good deal of freedom for movement and positioning; however, these two elements of drama become much more of an issue when a larger group is performing. Although much of the same attention to detail is required, there is also much more that can go wrong:

- Often you are not speaking or directly involved in the main action so you stop 'acting'.
- The audience can't see you because someone else is standing in front of you.
- You've been told not to worry about turning your back on the audience, but nobody can see your face – so how can you show your emotions?
- The whole movement of the group on stage looks clumsy and obviously 'rehearsed'.
- The audience doesn't know who to look at and what's important on stage.

To some extent, some of the above will disappear with simple familiarity with the script and what your movements are, so that where you stand becomes second nature. But much of the rest needs practice.

Group improvisation and space

In a group of four to six, develop a short piece of improvised or devised work based on the idea *Family at War*. This might be taken literally, for instance, a family living during a war. Or it might be a family at conflict over an issue or issues, perhaps a forthcoming marriage or the recent loss of a job. Or it might have some other interpretation of the theme.

1 Take up a position, or make a physical 'picture', which shows the whole family.

This can be at the start of the drama

or…

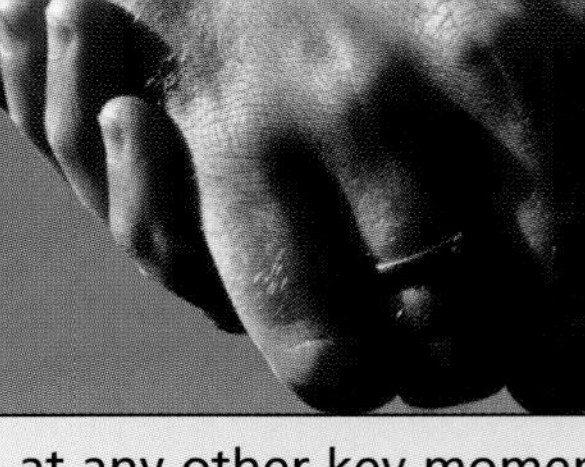

at any other key moment within it.

Then, in turn, each member of the group should step out of the 'picture' to look at the group – how they are seated, where they are standing, what the picture says about the family.

2 Now, as a group, work on seven to ten lines of dialogue from this same moment. You might like to write the lines down to help.

If you are stuck for inspiration, use these, taken from the idea, *Family at War*.

Shofiq:	I have to go back, mother.
Mother:	This is not our war. We live in England now.
Sister (*moves towards him*:)	You have a place at university – do you want to throw it away?
Shofiq:	Look, let me pack my bag. Let me go.
Brother:	If I was old enough, I would go.
Mother:	Don't say that. You should support me, help me to persuade him.
Shofiq:	This is my choice. I cannot stand by and watch our country being bombed. Don't you understand?
Mother:	All I understand is that you want to waste your life on a country you have never seen.

Each member of the group who speaks should decide:

- how they are going to respond to the line or action before they speak
- how they are going to behave after they have spoken.

For instance, in the case above:

- Will Shofiq continue packing his bag as he speaks?
- Will his brother stand near him? Behind him?
- Will his mother go up to him and touch him, try to prevent him? If so, where will they both stand?

Key Pointer!
Remember, a **simple gesture**, such as a light touch on the arm, is often more effective than any word or phrase.

Look at these two descriptions of moments from the dialogue on page 41. The lines being spoken are written beneath:

Description 1:

Shofiq is holding a bag open, filling it with food from the fridge.
His mother is standing nearby, her hand on his arm.
His younger brother (14) is behind them both, watching.
His sister is standing by the open kitchen door.

Line: I have to go back, mother.

Description 2:

Shofiq's sister is between him and the open door.

Line: You have a place at university – do you want to throw it away?

Discuss the problems with movement that might exist in this scene. Are there any? Could the characters remain where they are without moving?

These sorts of questions need to be applied to whatever drama you are performing. Some simple techniques can help – read what one drama student wrote about a production he saw citing the use of contrast.

> While the rest of the family laughed and chatted over drinks and snacks, Marty sat slumped in a chair without moving. His personal isolation from his family was emphasised by the director's decision to **physically** isolate him… and set him apart.

Visual plans/sketches

An actor does not want to be over-burdened with sketches or movement plans that have to be learned by heart, but in the practice stage it is helpful to get a sense of how moves can work. A simple sketch can help, even if it is discarded later.

1 Look at this plan. It shows the movements of Shofiq in the short dialogue above. The numbers refer to the lines of script, so [1] is his first line, [2] is his mother's and [3] is his sister's.

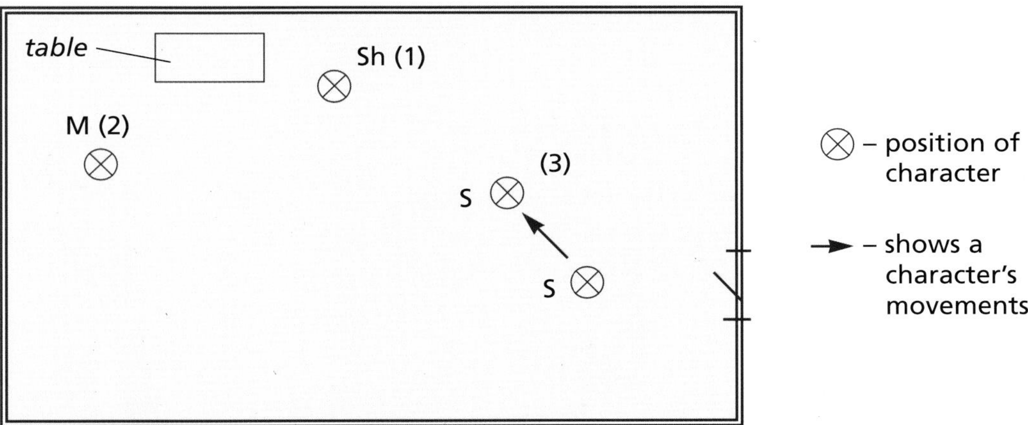

2 Now take any drama you are working on and draw a plan like the one above for one small section of text. Then run the performance with a group or partner and assess how well your suggested moves went.

A key is: **moving for purpose**. Don't simply move to get out of the way of another actor. What is the reason for the move – is it to threaten someone? To be intimate? To get a drink? To open a door? Is there another reason?

Commentary

Watch any performance piece by your class, or outside school or college.

Now write your own piece in which you focus entirely on the contrasts and other differences you observe in the various characters' positions and movements.
Use the following markers to help express your ideas:

- On the one hand…
- On the other…
- While…
- Similarly…
- However…
- In contrast…

Stillness

One other issue is the way in which, in an actor's haste to make sure he or she looks interesting, they overdo the acting with too many gestures and movements so that the audience never see any movement long enough for it to be caught in their minds.

Stillness can be a great gift to an actor. A common fault amongst amateur actors is that they cannot keep their feet in the same place and so they shift about restlessly, almost unconsciously.

Some 'still' exercises

On your own, do each of the following exercises in turn:

1. Decide on a single spot in the room. Walk to it, not too slowly, but not quickly. When you arrive, face the centre of the room and take up a still pose (not 'frozen') with feet planted in one place. Fold your arms. Hold the pose for five seconds.

2. Now, walk and find someone else in the room. Stop, and point out a place at the other side of the room. Concentrate on pointing and keeping your eyes fixed on that place. Hold it for five seconds.

3. Move to a chair, or other seating position within the room. Sit down, facing towards the middle, cross your legs and place your hands in a relaxed position in your lap. Don't look around the room. Look towards the centre for five seconds.

Now repeat all three exercises, but this time with half the class watching. Reverse the roles when finished so that the first half have a go.

Commentary

Who was able to remain still without looking 'frozen'? Who found it difficult to stay in one position, was fidgeting or turning round?

Practising stillness

In your group, read this extract from *An Inspector Calls*. In it, a police inspector is questioning the members of a family who may have been responsible, in a number of ways, for a young woman's death. In this scene he is questioning the mother of the family who, as the Chair of a charity committee, may have turned down the young woman's request for help and financial aid when she was pregnant. First of all, read it in fours without moving or standing, perhaps sitting in a circle.

An Inspector Calls by J B Priestley

Inspector (*to Mrs Birling*):	And you've nothing further to tell me?
Mrs Birling:	I'll tell you what I told her. Go and look for the father of the child. It's his responsibility.
Inspector:	That doesn't make it any the less yours. She came to you for help, at a time when no woman could have needed it more. And you not only refused it yourself but saw to it that the others refused it too. She was here alone, friendless, almost penniless, desperate. She needed not only money, but advice, sympathy, friendliness. You've had children. You must have known what she was feeling. And you slammed the door in her face.
Sheila (*with feeling*):	Mother, I think it was cruel and vile.
Birling (*dubiously*):	I must say, Sybil, that when this comes out at the inquest, it isn't going to do us much good. The Press might easily take it up...

Priestley's stage directions tell us that the Inspector "creates at once an impression of massiveness, solidity and purposefulness... He speaks carefully, weightily, and has a disconcerting habit of looking hard at the person he addresses before actually speaking". He is a naturally 'still' figure, a figure of authority and at the centre of things. So, where should he stand, or move, in relation to the rest of the cast?

1
2
3
4
5
6
7
8
9
10

1 Discuss these possibilities with your group:

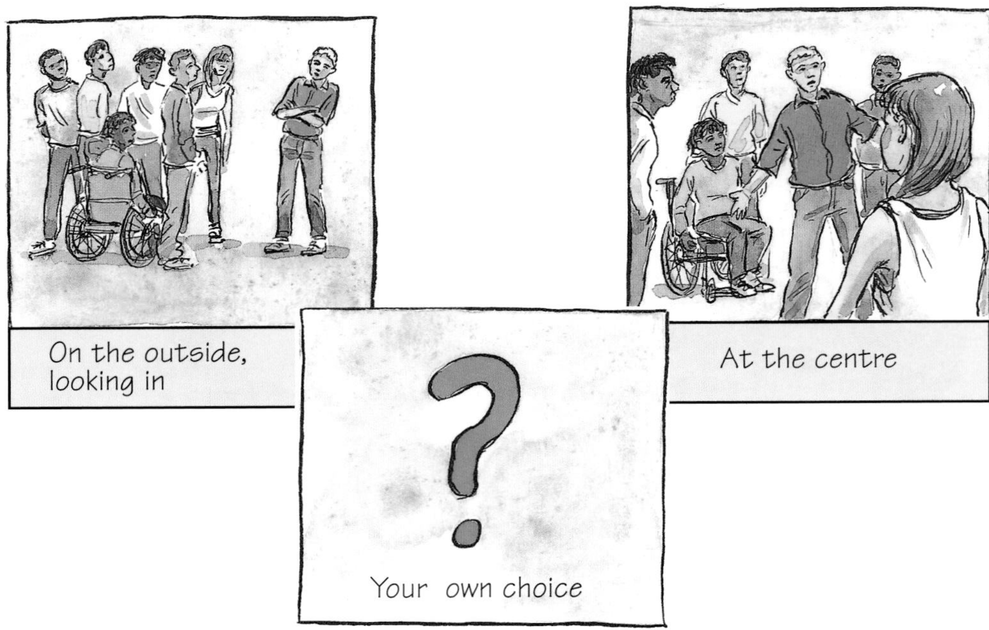

2 Now play the scene in two ways of your choice. Consider the whole idea of contrast – if the Inspector is very still and purposeful, how might the others behave?

Will the actor playing the Inspector follow Priestley's advice about how he looks hard at someone before speaking to them?

Add eye contact between the characters, perhaps between Mr Birling and his wife as he begins to get worried about her behaviour towards the young woman.

Commentary

1. Write a full account about what you have learned about movement and use of space by actors, commenting in particular on any texts you are working on, and how you might use the techniques you have studied. Refer to particular lines, as well as general comments about movement.

Read this student example, noting the italicised words which refer to movement.

> Roland Jeffrey twitches with jealousy as Leontes in The Winter's Tale at The New Arts Centre, Malding. At one point he stumbles to the front of the stage and points an accusing finger at me, in the front row, as if I had betrayed him! His lines are not so much spoken, as spat into his wife's face, from no more than an inch or two away, showing his abusive, uncontrolled nature. In contrast, Hermione is a model of serenity – still, and unmoved by her husband's madness.

Pace and tempo

It was once said that the only difference between hate and love on stage was speed. While this is a simplification, what it does show is that the pace at which a speech is delivered, or a scene is acted, can have a big effect on the meaning.

As a group, you are going to show a day-in-the-life of a station platform, a piece called *The train station.*

1 Divide up the following roles (adding others if you wish):

- cleaner with broom
- businessman or woman
- two friends
- tramp or beggar
- old woman or man
- parent/s and child/children
- station supervisor
- teenager with a huge stereo

2 Develop for your character/s a simple, fairly repetitive set of actions, but with no sounds. You can use fairly obvious clichés such as the one below, for the purposes of this:

Businessman:
Arrives
Sits down
Opens briefcase
Removes paper
Does crossword
Replaces paper
Closes case
Stands up
Moves up to train
Leaves

Practise your actions independently of other characters.

3 Now put all the actions together on the station platform, but in sequence. (The whole group, or teacher, will decide who comes in first, whether it is the cleaner at dawn or, perhaps, the station supervisor.)

4 Perform the piece again, but this time in 'real time'. Practise until the whole sequence is smooth and has a clear beginning and end (possibly with the cleaner at nightfall).

Changing pace

You are now going to play around with the pace.

5 Perform the sequence at breakneck speed (no one should run, but it should appear like a speeded-up film).
Then perform it in slow motion.

6 Finally, perform the sequence as follows:

Start in slow motion – halfway through move to breakneck speed – three-quarters of the way through go back to slow motion.

Commentary

Describe the process, the part you played and the overall effect of the finished piece. Were there any benefits from playing the sequence fast or slow? Did it make the daily, rather boring situation more interesting?

Applying pace to your acting

A piece of drama should have ebbs and flows, pace and pauses. Choosing where to speed up in an interchange or in a long speech is difficult and there are no easy answers. Try out what works best.

Take this scene, for instance:

Phil is in his house. He is slowly reading through a note left for him on the table. His movements are deliberate, heavy, as if his arms are leaden.

His brother or sister enters. With an effort he tries to brighten up, moving more quickly and trying to conceal the letter, and moves towards the work surface.

Phil: Want a cup of tea? I was just…

Lee: What was that you were reading?

Phil: Reading?

Lee: Yeah. The note.

Phil: Nothing.

Lee: Phil. Don't muck me around. There's something going on here – I want to know what it is.

Phil: It's not easy.

Lee: Get on with it. Spit it out.

There are many opportunities for playing around with the pace here. In pairs, read the scene through and then decide where and in what ways the pace can be altered according to what is being said and done.

Pace in longer pieces

One of the ways to maintain audience interest or to indicate an approaching moment of high drama or importance, is to create different pace throughout the play. On a simple level this might be represented by literally more action and movement on stage – characters come rushing in, lines are overlapped, answers come more quickly, speech is faster, gaps between entrances and exits are smaller – before following this by more measured speaking, longer silences and longer pauses.

A trapeze artist 'maintains audience interest'!

Commentary

Consider any longer play you have studied or acted in. Indicate on a line, like the one below, where the moments of pace should occur and, equally, the moments of slower action. Don't fall into the trap of assuming action is slow when a character has a long speech or monologue. These can still be energetic and pacy.

Add key moments above and below the graph line to show rise and fall in pace, and then draw lines between them.

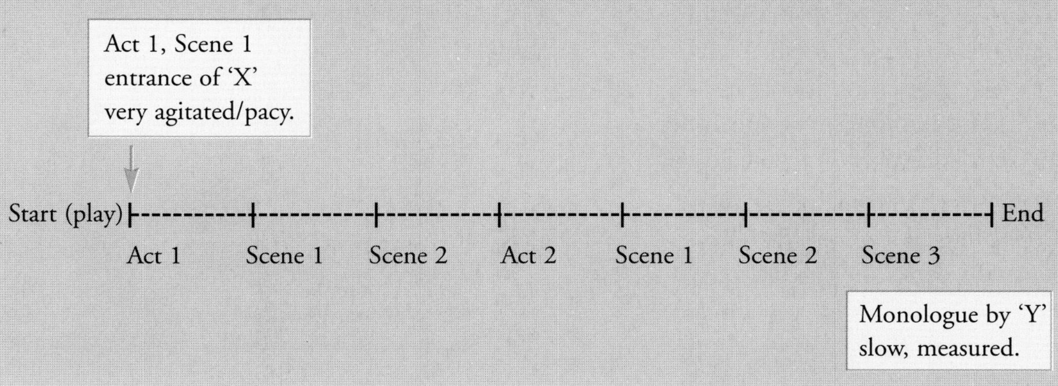

Perspective and focus

Now look at these three images of actors on stage.

1 Working with a friend, decide in each case which character the audience would focus on most. Discuss your reasons for your answers.

Of course, other factors would also have a big impact on the actor the audience watches:

- what has happened before (the history of the characters you are watching)
- the words, if any, being spoken
- the use of lighting, sound and other 'production' factors.

However, the framing of the actors on the stage, as in the three pictures, is a big factor in this. In each of the above, the poses are identical, as is the space between the figures.

2 Now, in pairs, experiment with these two body positions as shown in the pictures. Try five different combinations in the acting space. Initially, keep the same distance between you, but vary the angle and position from which the audience see you.

3 Now try five more positions, but this time alter the gap between you, as below.

4 Choose three of these angles and positions and show them to the rest of the group (who must remain in the same position as the audience).

Commentary

Ask the group what the effect was on:

- who they focused on
- what, if anything, it said about the relationship.

Audience position

In the Gods?

One other aspect which is often overlooked is the position of the audience. The same group of figures might be seen by the audience from an entirely different angle. They might be in front but high up and looking down directly on the actors in a fore-shortened view. Alternatively, they might be looking up at the stage from below (as in the front row of the stalls).

In many older theatres, the seats highest up, almost in the roof, are still referred to as 'the Gods'. Why is this an appropriate name for the audience sitting there, and how is it a different experience from those sitting in the front row?

Commentary

Write up your initial thoughts on the effect of framing on the stage, commenting on positions on the stage and the perspective of the audience. Write about any production you have seen, or been involved in, and comment on the effect of framing.

Using the eyes

Other factors, such as those mentioned earlier, can affect the way in which an audience views the action on stage. One element is the use of eyes. Take this image:

Where are the eyes looking? Look at the lines that have been added.

The Bacchae

Now look at the image on the right and imagine lines drawn from the eyes to the point they are drawing us towards.

Now take any image from a magazine, paper or advert and do the same exercise. It is particularly worthwhile with small groups.

Using the eyes in performance

5 In groups, set up a series of tableaux, *The Last Goodbye*. You could develop this from the work you did on page 41, *Family at War* or, alternatively, work with new material.

The Oedipus Trilogy

The group should consist of:

- mother
- father
- brother/sister
- boyfriend/girlfriend (of person leaving)
- person leaving

Using positioning and the direction the eyes are looking, try to show something about this leave-taking (for example, spurned love, hope for the future, etc.).

6 Show two or three tableaux to the rest of the class. They should comment on the effect of each and say what they can tell about the relationships.

Pair work

As in life, the way people use their eyes in relationships can be very telling. Although many stages are large and the use of the eyes is minimised, much drama takes place in smaller spaces.

In pairs, perform this short piece in the two ways suggested.

A cell. A lawyer on one side of the table. On the other, the condemned prisoner.

Prisoner: Well, what news?
Lawyer: It's not good I'm afraid.
Prisoner: What happened then?
Lawyer: The governor turned down your request.
Prisoner: What?
Lawyer: There's to be no appeal.
Prisoner: That's it then. I'm finished.
Lawyer: Yes. I'm sorry. We did all we could.

1 Play this with the lawyer looking directly at the prisoner without flinching.

2 Play it with the lawyer avoiding the eyes of the person opposite.

Commentary

In your pairs, discuss which of the two performances worked best. Then try some further interpretations, perhaps with a mixture of direct looking, looking away at key moments, and so on.

Make notes about how you could apply what you have looked at with regard to eyes to any other work or texts you are developing.

1
2
3
4
5
6
7
8
9
10

Objects and symbols

How performers pick up objects, open doors, sit down, eat food – the concrete elements of stage 'business' – are as important as the factors on the previous page in denoting character, relationships or in emphasising key issues of story or meaning.

At the end of William Shakespeare's *Hamlet*, a duel is fought in which one character has a poisoned tip on his sword and wine has been poisoned. The audience has complete knowledge – they even know that the swords have been switched so the 'wrong' person has the poisoned sword.

The poisoned wine has symbolic importance as it was poison that was used to commit the murder of Hamlet's father.

In such a case, the objects (sword and poisoned goblet) take on terrific significance, as agents of the story, as reminders of past events, and as symbols that the play is a revenge tragedy. However, objects do not have to be so obviously dramatic to have effect.

1 In groups, one of you should perform the following while the others watch.

You are entering a hallway. There is a pile of letters on the side. Amongst them is a letter from your wife or husband in an envelope saying she or he has left you. The audience knows the letter is in the pile.

Play the scene in these three ways:
- Casually flick through the letters before putting them down again.
- Flick through the letters, pause briefly on the one addressed to you, but put them down again.
- Flick through the letters, start opening 'the one', then be distracted by something else.

Make sure that you don't show you, the actor, know the significance of the letter.

Now play the scene as if you know the letter is there:
- Enter the hallway and pick up the letters.
- Look through them quickly until you find the one you expect.

Show clearly that you know the significance of the letter.

2 Then, as a group, develop the drama by introducing the consequences and other characters.

Slow-time and objects

One of the difficulties of stage work is that time on stage cannot usually be real-time. If you want the audience to be aware of what is happening, there sometimes needs to be deliberation in the way you handle objects, open doors, etc. If it is too lazy, casual or quick, the action can be missed.

1 Try this seemingly simple exercise, working with one chair only and no other props.

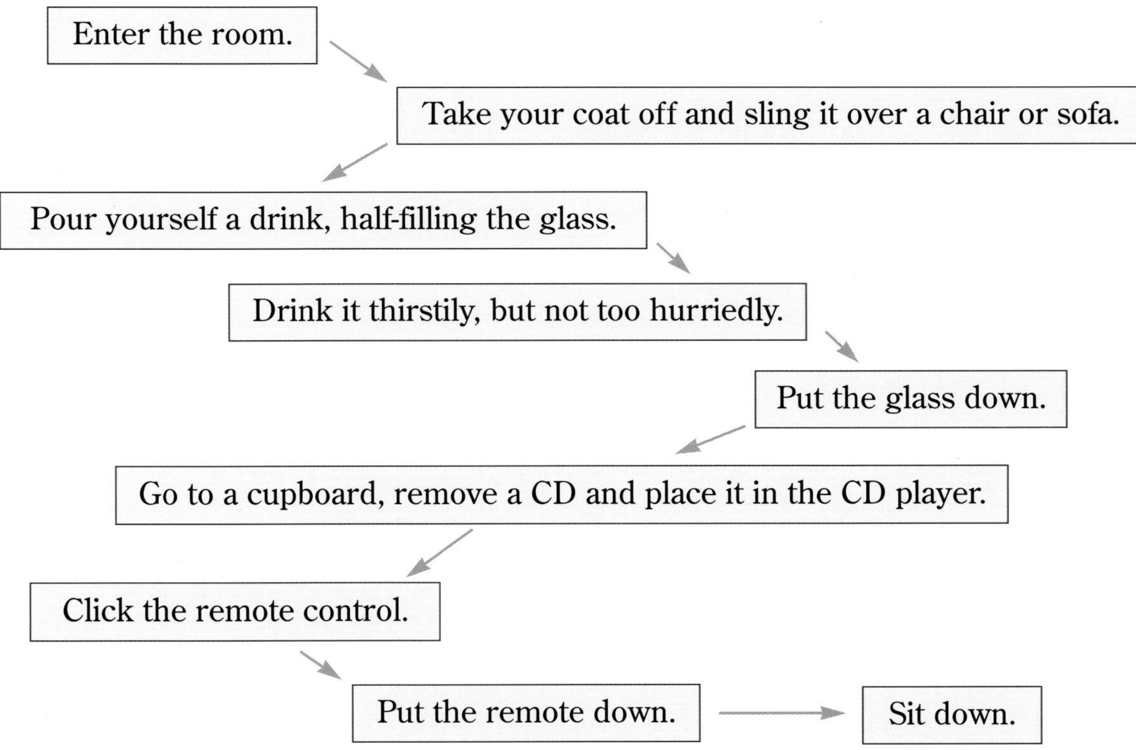

Ask a partner to watch your performance, then comment on how effectively you portrayed the different moves. Which elements do you have to slow down; which do you need to make more obvious?

2 Finally, perform it again with your partner's suggestions incorporated.

5 Words

In this chapter you will look at:

- *the power of words on stage*
- *rhythms and patterns of language*
- *words and character.*

1
2
3
4
5
6
7
8
9
10

The language of life

Language on stage can take many forms, for example:

- the powerful soliloquy or monologue spoken by one character
- rapid interplay of short lines between a number of characters
- the short 'aside' spoken as if to the audience and not intended for the ears of the other characters
- long, reflective conversations.

However, what is said – the actual words spoken – varies enormously. As there are variations in the language we use in life, so there are variations in the language chosen by playwrights and acting companies.

1 In English lessons you will have discussed the different genres and styles which language can take. As a short improvisational reminder, work in pairs on the following activity. Below is a list of 'language situations'. One of you, A, should begin by speaking in the style given, but after several seconds B (the other) should take over or interrupt.

Make sure the seven styles are very distinct. Think about:

- your choice of words
- any accent or emphasis you might give, etc.

Begin:

A A woman dictating a business letter to her secretary about an important meeting.

B A newsreader revealing the birth of a new child for the Royal family.

A The voice-over for an advert trying to sell a new brand of sexy perfume.

B A motor-racing commentator describing a spectacular crash.

A A voice narrating the start of a horror story on radio.

B Someone explaining their innermost thoughts about a relationship that's gone wrong.

A A mechanic explaining what is wrong with an old banger to a gullible customer.

Commentary

With your partner, briefly discuss which of these was the most difficult to perform. You may find that part of the reason might be lack of knowledge about how such a person might speak.

1 2 3 4 5 6 7 8 9 10

Language in scripts

When you see speech written on the page, much of it can appear unnatural, forced or stylised. Yet when the words are spoken on stage, they can come alive and make complete sense.

Read these two examples of play language:

Maria Marten, or the Murder in the Red Barn (a traditional story)

This passage is taken from a Victorian melodrama *Maria Marten*. Maria is talking about the father of her child, a man who has betrayed her and who will ultimately kill her.

Maria: Another day passes and he comes not. Oh, my child, my child, would that thy heartbroken mother and thyself could sink to sleep and peace for ever. Twelve months this day I was a happy village girl. Today what am I? A betrayed, a ruined woman, thus scorned of all who knew my shame.

Dealer's Choice by Patrick Marber

This extract comes from Dealer's Choice by Patrick Marber. Mugsy is trying to persuade Sweeney to join in their regular game of poker which their boss organises once a month.

1 2 3 4 5 6 7 8 9 10

Sweeney: I can't play.

Mugsy: We know that.

Sweeney makes a fake laugh.

Mugsy: Why can't you play?

Beat.

Sweeney: I'm seeing Louise.

Mugsy: You're seeing a dolly bird?

Sweeney: Louise.

Dealer's Choice

Mugsy: Louise?

Sweeney: My kid you prat.

Mugsy: I thought your missus wouldn't let you see her?

Sweeney: Well, I'm seeing her tomorrow, special dispensation.

Mugsy: Tomorrow's tomorrow, you can play tonight.

Sweeney: I haven't seen my kid for three months, you could at least pretend to be pleased.

Mugsy smiles grotesquely.

Sweeney: One dark night some deaf, dumb and blind old hag will present you with a child, a little fat gurgling mini Mugsy, then you'll understand responsibility.

Mugsy: And what about your responsibility to poker?

Putting aside the subject matter, clearly there is a difference in the form of language.

1 Discuss which extract, 1 or 2:

- is conversational and chatty
- uses exaggerated language to describe real emotions
- has mostly short, punchy lines
- uses longer, more complex sentences
- sounds natural
- sounds artificial.

Only one section from extract 2, *Dealer's Choice*, could be considered similar to the *Maria Marten* extract. It is the mini-speech by Sweeney starting, "One dark night… ".

2 In pairs, play the scene from *Dealer's Choice*. Whoever plays Sweeney should read that mini-speech differently from the other lines. Try saying it as if you are trying to create a picture of this situation in the air for the audience – of Mugsy being presented with a child. Try looking away from Mugsy out towards the audience.

Now try saying it in the same style as the other lines – for instance naturally, as if it's a 'throwaway' remark, unimportant.

3 Now look at the speech by Maria. In how many different ways can this be spoken? On your own, try reading it in each of the following styles:

1 Dreadfully upset, almost in tears.

2 Upset, but also angry.

3 Quizzical – anxious, slightly bemused, as if she doesn't quite understand what is happening.

Commentary

Make notes on both these extracts. Say whether there is a 'proper' way they should be spoken, or to what extent anything goes. Could Maria's speech be spoken with giggles and laughter? Try it out if you're not sure – the effect might be quite interesting!

Language that conceals

Traditionally, you will have been used to language being a key to 'character', to looking inside someone's mind and understanding their motives. In short, being able to empathise with them. However, this does not always happen. Sometimes language is the play – and we find little out about the characters behind the words.

Read this extract from Harold Pinter's play *Mountain Language*.

Mountain Language, by Harold Pinter

OFFICER (to **YOUNG WOMAN**)
Any complaints?

YOUNG WOMAN
She's been bitten.

OFFICER
Who?

Pause.

Who? Who's been bitten?

WOMAN
She has. She has a torn hand. Look. Her hand has been bitten. This is blood.

SERGEANT (To **YOUNG WOMAN**)
What is your name?

OFFICER
Shut up.

He walks over to **ELDERLY WOMAN**

What's happened to your hand? Has someone bitten your hand?

The **WOMAN** *slowly lifts her hand. He peers at it.*

Who did this? Who bit you?

YOUNG WOMAN
A Dobermann pinscher.

OFFICER
Which one?

Pause.

Which one?

Pause.

Sergeant!

SERGEANT *steps forward.*

SERGEANT
Sir!

OFFICER
Look at this woman's hand. I think the thumb is going to come off. (*To* **ELDERLY WOMAN**) Who did this?

She stares at him.

Who did this?

YOUNG WOMAN
A big dog.

OFFICER
What was his name?

Pause.

What was his *name*?

Pause.

Every dog has a *name*! They answer to their name. They are given a name by their parents and that is their name, that is their *name*! Before they bite, they *state* their name. It's a formal procedure. They state their name and then they bite. What was his name? If you tell me one of our dogs bit this woman without giving his name I will have that dog shot!

Silence.

Now – attention! Silence and attention! Sergeant!

SERGEANT
Sir?

OFFICER
Take any complaints.

In fours, read through this scene aloud. The fourth person, playing 'elderly woman', can listen for the moment.

Describing the language

Here are some statements that could be made about the extract:

1 No characters have names.

2 They have roles – Officer, Sergeant, Young Woman, etc.

3 The situation is familiar – some form of military people in charge of prisoners.

4 There is aggression in the extract.

5 There is also, possibly, humour.

6 Most of the language seems everyday, recognisable – almost normal, but some of the turns of phrase seem a little strange.

7 The language takes a sudden ridiculous turn at one point; but it is also frightening.

8 The language is strongly repetitive.

1 In your groups, look at points 1 to 8. Find examples of each of these statements.

2 Reread the scene, but this time add movements. It is not a long scene so, if possible, try to practise it until you no longer need the script.

Pay close attention to:

- the punctuation (the short sentences)
- the pauses (decide what actions, if any, are going on at this time)
- the violence of the Officer's longer speech at the end and the effect it has.

Practise the scene until you feel you have got just the right balance of aggression and strangeness, but also everydayness.

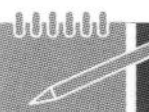

Commentary

Here is one student's written commentary about the language of the extract. Read it and then write about your own work, and how the language either helps or hinders the performers. Also, write about the mood created by the language, as well as the interplay between the characters, and how much Pinter allows us to find out about them.

> Rehearsing this scene it was clear that trying to find out the usual things about the characters was difficult. 'Young Woman' told us nothing. I was playing her, but I didn't know her name, her background. She could have been any young woman. All she does is give information in simple phrases; 'She's been bitten'. She only speaks when she is spoken to – but this is probably what it's like for prisoners-of-war. I tried to bring this out by making her say what she had to say, but not try to upset the officers. But I also wanted to make her look a little defiant, as she does complain when she has the chance. So, I made her look directly in the Officer's eyes.

Taking the language forward

3 Having worked on the script in your group, now take the language and play forward. Improvise a further scene from the piece – or take it to its logical conclusion.

However, don't think about 'plot' or 'story'. Instead, develop scenes which feature the same characters, or even new ones, using similar language. The links between these scenes can be very thin, with no obvious connection.

Possible scenes could be:

- a one-to-one interrogation
- the old woman's story
- outside the prison walls
- the people from the mountain
- the Officer's story.

These could be developed through:

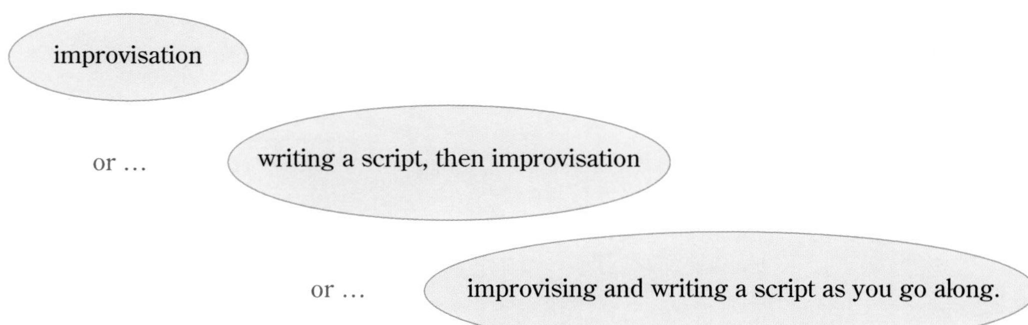

Performing more scenes from *Mountain Language*

4 Perform your final piece. You might wish to begin with the original Pinter script and add your scenes afterwards.

Commentary

Discuss how well you were able to imitate and continue the language. If you weren't successful, what elements do you need to change?

The power of words

A person walks into a space and says:
I want to tell you a story. Once upon a time…

A person walks into a space and says:
The end.
... and walks off again.

A person walks into a space and says:
… nothing.

The person stays sitting there.

Each of these expressions – the familiar, the unexpected, the silent – are possible, and all have dramatic possibility. The words, or lack of them, create questions:

- What is the story? Is it one I know? These words are known to me from childhood. Will this be a fairy story?
- If this is the end, what was the beginning? Why is the 'end' first?
- When is he going to speak? Why is he silent? What will be the first word he says?
- Why is he sitting there? What is he waiting for?

Without the space and the man, however, the words are meaningless.

Making meanings

Read these words aloud:

Never, never, never, never, never!

1 Work in pairs. Say them to each other. Try to invest them with some meaning. Create a situation in your mind, but do not tell you partner what it is. Have the words come to life?

The words come from the end of Shakespeare's *King Lear*. The old king holds his murdered daughter in his arms, and has laid a feather against her lips to see if she still breathes. His words are confirmation that she is dead.

The play has begun with Lear rejecting his daughter because she won't flatter him. His two other daughters, however, later betray him. Cordelia remains faithful, but she dies before he is reconciled with her.

2 In pairs, work first at one of you holding the other's body up, as in the picture below – or sitting alongside the body laid on the ground, until you feel comfortable with the truthfulness of the pose.

Now add the likely gestures of the old king. Perhaps:

- placing his ear to his daughter's lips
- placing his hands above her mouth to feel any breath
- any other movement such as looking for a pulse.

Now add the words. Decide whether:

- they are said in one go, or as separate responses to each attempt to find life
- they are said in some other way, perhaps as a series of statements to the assembled onlookers. Perhaps he waits until he is sure she is dead before he gets up and moves away?

3 Show your completed performance to the rest of the group.

4 Discuss how each one is different. Focus, in particular, on the different individual gestures, movements and decisions about how to say the line. Which worked best?

Commentary

Write a description of this work. Describe in as clear detail as possible your presentation of this line, and then several others you saw. Identify what worked, and why.

The single voice

Many productions feature moments when the audience focuses on the single voice, the moment when the actor speaks at great length – perhaps on his or her own, with no one on stage, or while all the other performers stand and listen.

Here, while we may be aware of the actor's movements – or stillness – it is the words that we concentrate on. But how, as a performer, can you bring out all the different elements of a longer speech?

This extract comes from the opening to *The Cherry Orchard* by Anton Chekhov. It is set in Russia.

David Troughton as Lopakhin in a production by the Royal Shakespeare Company.

The Cherry Orchard by Anton Chekhov

Lopakhin, a businessman, is in the room known as the Nursery, with Dunyasha, the maid of the house. They are awaiting the arrival of Ranyevskaya, the woman who owns the house, and her family. They have been away for five years. Lopakhin had intended to meet them at the station, but fell asleep.

Lopakhin *(carrying a book)*:

She's lived abroad for five years – I don't know what she'll be like now... She's a fine woman. Easy, straightforward. I remember, when I was a boy of fifteen or so, my father – he kept a shop then in the village here – dead now, of course – he punched me in the face, and the blood started to pour out of my nose... For some reason we'd come into the yard here together, and he was drunk. It seems like yesterday. She was only young – such a slim young thing. She brought me in and she took me to the washstand in this room, in the nursery.

'Don't cry, my little peasant,' she says. 'It'll heal in time for your wedding... '

Pause.

My little peasant... it's true, my father was a peasant – and here am I in a white waistcoat and yellow shoes. Like a pig in a pastry-cook's ... The only difference is I'm a rich man, plenty of money, but look twice and I'm a peasant, a real peasant... (*Leafs through the book.*) I was reading this book. Couldn't understand a word. Fell asleep over it.

1 Read this speech quietly to yourself, or speak it out loud on your own, in your own time.

2 Now look at this chart starting to plot the 'movement' of the speech:

Line	Purpose
1	Information, then wondering what she'll be like.
2–9	Describing Ranyevskaya; remembering the incident with his father, etc.

Continue the chart. There's no need to write it down, but decide mentally what each line or new sentence is doing (perhaps it is describing someone or expressing regret).

Performing

Now look at this annotated version of the same speech. This is not the only way to play it, but will give you some idea of the possible changes in emphasis from phrase to phrase.

Shrugs his shoulders, as if unsure

1. She's lived abroad for five years – I don't know what she'll be like now... She's a fine woman. Easy, straightforward. I remember, when I was a boy of fifteen or so, my father – he kept a shop then in the village here – dead now, of course – he punched me in the face, and the blood started to pour out of my nose... For some reason we'd come into the yard here together, and he was drunk. It seems like yesterday. She was only young – such a slim young thing. She brought me in and she took me to the washstand in this room, in the nursery.

Moving to window

Disgusted at memory

Puts on the voice of a gentle mother

'Don't cry, my little peasant,' she says. 'It'll heal in time for your wedding... '

Pause.

10. My little peasant... it's true, my father was a peasant – and here am I in a white waistcoat and yellow shoes. Like a pig in a pastry-cook's... The only difference is I'm a rich man, plenty of money, but look twice and I'm a peasant, a real peasant... (*Leafs through the book.*) I was reading this book. Couldn't understand a word. Fell asleep over it.

As if he's ridiculous

There's much that you can add here – the movements, the change in pace, emphasis, etc., but the manner in which you say these words is one way of breaking this speech into a series of mini-speeches or mini-segments that will make it come alive for the audience.

3 Practise and perform the speech to your group, or the rest of the class. Remember to have Dunyasha present, so that Lopakhin has someone to 'play off'.

Commentary

When you have finished, write up how you broke the speech down, and what you did at key moments within it.

Using verse

Reading a poem or verse aloud is one way of focusing entirely on words. Every poem read aloud is a sort of play with many of the same ingredients.

The reader is not the poet	The actor is not the character
The words are by the poet	The words are by the playwright
The audience watch and listen	The audience watch and listen

To focus on the impact of individual lines and words, start by choosing one of the lines or phrases from the list below.

If you want to breathe…

… a cobweb on the cave of your dreams

Throw away the key

Forget everything

If you want to think…

1 Now, on your own, take your chosen line and read it aloud to yourself, perhaps as you walk around the class. Say it as often as is required until you find the words seem 'comfortable' on your lips. Try different ways of saying the words by:

- stressing different syllables
- changing the pitch and volume
- speaking in a particular tone.

2 Now move into a whole group or class situation and sit in a circle. One person in the group should read the whole poem below aloud, but as it comes to the line or phrase you decided upon, say it out loud – together with the others in your group who chose the same line.

Listen to Me

If you want to speak
your punishment is death.
If you want to breathe
your place is in the prison.
If you want to walk
then cut off your legs
and carry them in your arms.
If you want to laugh
hang upside down in a well.
If you want to think
then shut all the doors
and throw away the key.
If you want to cry
then sink into the river.
If you want to live
then become a cobweb on the cave
of your dreams.
And if you want to forget everything
then pause and think:
of the word you first learnt.

Kishwar Naheed

Discuss in the whole group:

- What effect, if any, did spending time on those previous chosen lines or phrases have?
- What are the powerful words or phrases in this? Are they the same ones as those on page 68? Or do others stand out?
- Without trying to fill in a background story, what different voices or tones can you pick out (for instance, bitter, pleading, defiant, joyful)?

3 Finally, take the verse away and prepare your own reading. Say each line or phrase in turn, as you did with the first one you chose, until each line has its own sound and meaning.

Commentary

Describe the 'character' in the poem in your own words. Use the same description you would use for a character on stage.

From poem to monologue

It is very difficult to explain the impact of individual words, phrases or speeches unless they are part of the whole play. On their own, they mean little. However, put them in context and the words become very powerful, even when the effect, as in the extract below, is intended to be humorous.

This extract comes from Aphra Behn's *The Rover*, a Restoration comedy from the mid-seventeenth century. In this scene, Blunt, a rather innocent 'countryman' from Essex, is emerging from a sewer having been tricked by his 'friends' who lured him into a lady's bedchamber making him think she was interested in him, before throwing him through a trap-door, naked, into the filth below. As you read it, don't worry too much about the meaning of the words – just try to get the emotion and the feeling in them.

The Rover by Aphra Behn

The Scene changes and discovers Blunt, *creeping out of a Common Shore, his Face, &c., all dirty.*

Blunt: Oh Lord! *(Climbing up)*
I am got out at last, and (which is a Miracle) without a Clue – and now to Damning and Cursing, – but if that would ease me, where shall I begin? With my Fortune, my self, or the Quean that cozen'd me – What a dog was I to believe in Women! Oh Coxcomb – ignorant conceited Coxcomb! to fancy she cou'd be enamour'd with my Person, at the first sight enamour'd – Oh, I'm a curs'd Puppy, 'tis plain, Fool was writ upon my Forehead, she perceiv'd it, – saw the *Essex* Calf there – for what Allurements could there be in this Countenance? which I can indure, because I'm acquainted with it – Oh, dull, silly Dog! to be thus sooth'd into a Cozening! Had I been drunk, I might fondly have credited the young Quean! but as I was in my right Wits, to be thus cheated, confirms I am a dull believing *English* Country Fop.

Cozen	cheat or deceive
Coxcomb	foolish, vain man
Enamoured	in love with
Allurements	attractions
Countenance	face

Commentary

In a monologue, the character is sharing his true feelings with the audience. Explain, with reference to the text, how Blunt feels, and how you could show this in your performance.

Character

6

In this chapter you will:

- *explore what 'character' means*
- *become clear about the key elements that make a successful character*
- *put those elements into practice.*

1 2 3 4 5 6 7 8 9 10

What is character?

In your work you will probably come across two main forms of characterisation:

- The first is the creation of a character of your own, not from a direct written playscript but through improvisation or other stimuli.
- The second is the interpretation of a character created by someone else, probably a playwright in a written script.

Preparation and presentation

The skills required in developing these two areas are very similar, but not identical.

Preparation	**Presentation and performance** *The skills here may well form the main part of your practical assessment.*
Here are some of the ways that preparation may be judged: • insight and accuracy • identification of problems • commitment and imagination • exploration of motivations and relationships • knowledge of methods and techniques • sensitivity to rest of acting group • understanding and research into the role.	Here are some of the ways your performance may be judged: • your insight and credibility (how believable the role is) and how relevant • how well you are able to sustain the role (keep it going) • how well you demonstrate performing skills and techniques • your commitment to the group and performance • your imagination • your originality and flair (ability to bring something different and new to the character or role).

Definitions of 'character'

We often use the word 'character' quite loosely to describe the sorts of people who appear in a play, film or story. For example, these are both characters from plays:

Hamlet: Prince of Denmark, tortured son of a murdered King

Romeo: star-struck teenager doomed to a tragic end

These definitions are common ones, but not necessarily the only ones.

Even playwrights, however, vary enormously in the amount of information and number of clues they provide. Sometimes a cast list is all that is given, with perhaps a single phrase.
For example:

Romeo *son to Montague* or Shylock *a rich Jew*

On other occasions, there is more detail given, perhaps in the opening scene directions. For example, read this extract from *Time and the Conways* by J B Priestley:

> CAROL, the youngest of the Conways – perhaps sixteen – and now terrifically excited, breathless, and almost tottering beneath a load of charade stuff, including a cigar-box gloriously filled with old false whiskers and noses, spectacles, and what not. With all the reckless haste of a child she bangs down all this stuff, and starts to talk, although she has no breath left.

Priestley adds the comment that Carol is an 'enchanting young person' but that from now on the characters can be left to 'explain themselves'.

Using stage directions

1 On your own, look at Priestley's stage directions and practise Carol's entrance. Key words to bear in mind are:

- terrifically excited
- almost tottering
- reckless haste of a child
- enchanting.

Describing characters

2 Now, in your groups, share your performances. Was everyone's the same? What differences did you notice? Were these differences deliberate or accidental?

Of course, although it appears that Priestley has left little room for the actor to add her own ideas, little touches can make each performance different – after all, there are degrees of 'reckless haste'.

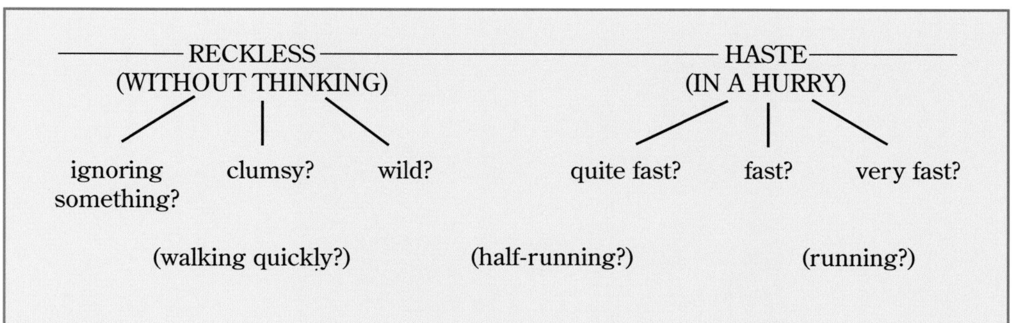

Here are some possibilities to try when you perform. Some will emphasise what Priestley says, others alter it slightly:

- Try laughing or giggling as you enter.
- Try almost dropping the box (real or imaginary) and just catching it.
- Try running in, which seems implied by the text but isn't actually mentioned.

Did this brief work give you a sense of what Carol is really like?

Of course, as an actor you would do far more than base your characterisation on the opening stage directions.

Commentary

Here is how one student described an actress playing Rita in Willy Russell's play *Educating Rita.*

> With her quick, **bird-like** movements Rita **pecks away** at Frank's cynical and world-weary facade. She seems to hop around the stage, peering into this and that, **like a curious sparrow**, while Frank watches her, **like a fat, lazy cat**, not quite sure whether to squash her, or admire her impudence.

One aspect of the description has been highlighted – the use of simile and metaphor to describe Rita's movement and Frank's immobility. Choose a character from the list below and see if you can write a paragraph about him or her in a similar style:

- an actor from a television soap opera you know well
- an actor from a production you have seen recently
- an actor from a film you have seen recently.

Here are two well-known actresses describing characters they have played. Firstly, Pam St Clement describes the role of Pat Butcher in *EastEnders* in *Sheer Bloody Magic*.

Pam St Clement

> Pat in *EastEnders* is certainly no softie. I first came into *EastEnders* in May 1986, eighteen months after it had started. Playing Pat is a bit like wearing an old sock really. I've got used to wearing her now. I didn't come in as a regular, I came in for a few episodes to create turmoil – which indeed I did. Having done that and been a real, venomous bitch to my ex-husband's then current wife, I disappeared back to the man I was living with, Mr Wicks...
>
> ... I did cause havoc at first but I've been very lucky with the character because I've slowly been allowed to develop it. Pat is very streetwise and very protective of her own, very defensive because she is vulnerable. She's vulnerable because she has been used by men, mostly. Or hasn't chosen the men for the right reasons. I have a suspicion that Pat was probably put on the wrong track in her youth and, brought up in the fifties and sixties, probably suffered from peer group pressure.

Here, Judi Dench talks about playing unsympathetic roles.

Dame Judi Dench

> I don't mind playing unsympathetic characters at all. I longed, for example, to play Regan*. I don't particularly want sympathy for my character unless that's the intention of the author. I think it's good to try and make things work, but you can't just come on being a villain from the beginning. People are not like that. We're all so multi-layered that it's only worth trying to find those layers so that you *see* this person – and I don't mean to excuse them in any kind of way. What I like to show is the *reason* for this person being the way they are – 'this is the formula for this person'.

*Regan is one of the daughters in Shakespeare's *King Lear*.)

There are a number of things you can perhaps learn from these two extracts.

Being the character

Firstly, the way Pam St Clement slips in and out of referring to Pat Butcher as 'I' ('I caused havoc… ') which suggests she almost thinks of herself as the character. You cannot do this in quite the same way in a few weeks of rehearsal, but it is often useful to refer to the character you are playing as 'I' rather than 'he' or 'she'.

1 Describe any character you have played, or are playing, to your partner for two minutes, referring to him or her as 'I'.

The 'formula'

Do you understand the character you are playing? Pam St Clement invents a childhood for hers and Judi Dench talks about the 'formula' – the many layers that make up a character.

2 Describe yourself in this way. Talk about your 'layers'. Perhaps you have an outer coat that people see, but you're different inside; perhaps you behave differently with different people.

A recipe for character?

There are many, many ways actors build character from the lines on a page, or from improvisation. Depending on opinion, some are considered more successful than others, but we will treat each method as equal and try them out. The following examples deal mainly with written characters in plays.

You can apply the following to any character you need to.

1 Personal knowledge

What do we know about them?
Consider:

- How old are they?
- What are we told about their relationships (with brothers, sisters, widows, etc.)?
- What do they say about themselves, and what do others say and do towards them?
- Do we know what they look like and what they wear? 
- Do they have a particular social standing (perhaps a job)?
- What do they want? What is their MOTIVE (see page 78)?
- Do they have a particular STATUS (see page 80) in relation to the other characters (are they weak or strong, etc.)?

2 Plot knowledge

What 'journey', if any, does this character make in the play? What is his or her personal story (which may or may not be the main story of the play)? Consider:

- What are the circumstances of their first entrance (when and where do we first meet them)?
- Why do they first appear in the story?
- Which key scene or scenes throughout the play are they involved in and when?
- What are the circumstances of their last appearance?
- What contribution to the story do they have, or what effect?

3 Historical/social knowledge

What do we know about the time and culture of this play and the world this character inhabits (for example, is he a stallholder in an Elizabethan market?)? What sort of life did a man, woman or child like our character have at this time in 'real life'?

Is their life in the play very different, or similar?

4 Empathy

Given what I know about the character, his or her 'journey' and motives, and the background to the play, is there any common ground where I can relate to the character's feelings or behaviour?

For example, do they experience:

- a moment of great joy or sadness
- a moment of conflict
- a key relationship.

Or do they demonstrate a particular way of behaving, or quirk of character? If so, can you share any of these things in some way?

Commentary

There are some people who feel this in-depth approach to character is unnecessary and that the words on the page should be enough. Nothing should be invented, or imagined, and it is not necessary to 'empathise' with a character to play them convincingly.

What do you think? To what extent do the lists above help you to establish and build a character?

Motive and status

Two of the aspects mentioned above which often help in establishing character are: **motive** and **status**.

Motive can mean:
- why someone behaves in the way they do (the formula)
- what his or her intentions are at a particular moment in the play, or the play as a whole.

Motives can be:
- on the surface
- hidden
- known to the character
- unknown to the character
- known to the audience
- unknown to the audience.

1 Read this simple dialogue.

Eddie: I lost my temper – I shouldn't have.

Dina: No – you shouldn't.

Eddie: It's just… things build up, get too much.

Dina: I know.

Thought tracking

The thoughts going on 'behind' these words can have a big impact on how the lines are played. For example, in pairs, perform these lines with these motives:

Eddie: I lost my temper – I shouldn't have.
(He wants to say 'sorry', but can't quite make a full apology)

Dina: No – you shouldn't.
(She wants him to know forgiveness won't come easily)

Eddie: It's just… things build up, get too much.
(He wants to tell her how he feels, but also wants to be 'let off', excused for his actions)

Dina: I know.
(She still wants to make it hard, but also wants to show she is softening)

Trying different motives

2 Of course, what a character wants, in exactly the same way as an ordinary person, can be hidden to themselves – or is not expressed by their words, for example:

Dina: I want you to leave.
(I want him to believe that, but really I'd rather he stayed)

Eddie: Don't worry – I'm going.
(I have no intention of going – I can still make it up to her)

Now try running the scene with different motives or 'wants' at each point of dialogue. Decide before you perform what those motives are.

Difficulties

In a novel, unlike a play, we could see inside what the characters are thinking. For example, Dina's motives might be:

I told Eddie I wanted him to go, and sat down on the sofa. The truth is, I hoped he'd protest, sit down next to me, tell me he loved me again.

So how do we show inner feelings on stage? The truth is, it is only possible by having established Dina's character beforehand. Earlier in the action she might have said:

"I know he's wrong for me, but I can't let him go."

Or…

"He's got me twisted round his little finger."

Both of these lines would help set up the situation you have played above.

Commentary

Write a thought-track, like the one above, for any scene of your own choice, or take a speech from a play-scene and transform it into a short prose extract from a novel.

Status

When we talk about the 'status' or 'power' of a character within a scene, or whole play, we are not necessarily talking about whether one character literally has power (for example, a king over a servant, a parent over a child), but about the way the relationships work.

For example, in the scene above:

GENERALLY
Eddie has power over Dina – she finds it almost impossible to end the relationship with him.

SPECIFICALLY (in this scene)
Dina might be seen to be more powerful. She is apparently controlling the situation; she can choose to forgive him, choose to make him suffer for what he's done. But Eddie can seize 'power' back by agreeing to leave, rather than appearing to argue and fight.

Power and status can therefore shift almost line by line.

1 Look at this new scene between Eddie and Dina. Dina has met someone else. She genuinely doesn't need Eddie anymore, but she feels a little guilty.

Eddie:	I'll get my things.
Dina:	Take your time – no need to hurry…
Eddie:	Thought you'd want me out of the way?
Dina:	Don't be childish. We can still be…
Eddie:	Friends? That old line.
Dina:	Civilised. We don't have to fight.
Eddie:	Yes – we'll be grown-up and civilised. In fact, let's pretend none of this ever happened.
Dina:	No need to be like that.
Eddie:	Why not? I know everything's my fault – the way I treated you. You never got to see the best of me…
Dina:	Eddie – don't… things weren't always bad.
Eddie:	No? Look, forget it. Forget me. I've got my stuff. I'll soon be history.
Dina:	I'm sorry, Eddie. Sorry I met someone else. But you can't blame me. You never really wanted me. The truth is, when you walk through that door, you'll hardly give me another thought. It's over – and it's best this way.

Shifting power

2 In pairs, read the scene aloud carefully, looking at the shifting power within it. Focus on Eddie's words of 'emotional blackmail', his efforts to arouse sympathy from Dina. Then play the scene in pairs. Think about how the power might shift back towards Dina in her last speech.

Other things to consider are:

- How will the characters' movements reflect their states of mind?
- What are they actually doing – is Eddie collecting his CDs?
- What are Eddie and Dina thinking; what are their motives?
- Does Eddie genuinely want Dina to change her mind?
- Does Dina care about what Eddie feels? Does she really want him to take his time?

One way of practising status and seeing how far you can push the boundaries of who is in control is to assign a number between 1 and 10 to each character (10 = highest power or status, 1 = lowest). Try the scene – or any other scene between two characters – applying the following status levels.

a) 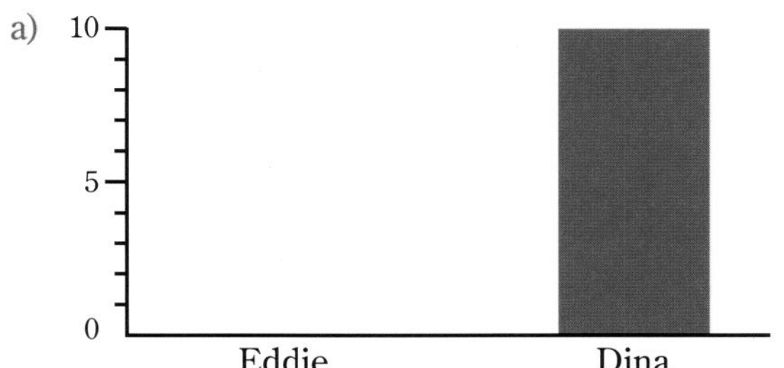

Eddie: no status, little power. Could be played as subdued, quiet, etc.

Dina: high status. Could be played as if she really doesn't care, wants Eddie off her hands immediately despite what she says.

b) 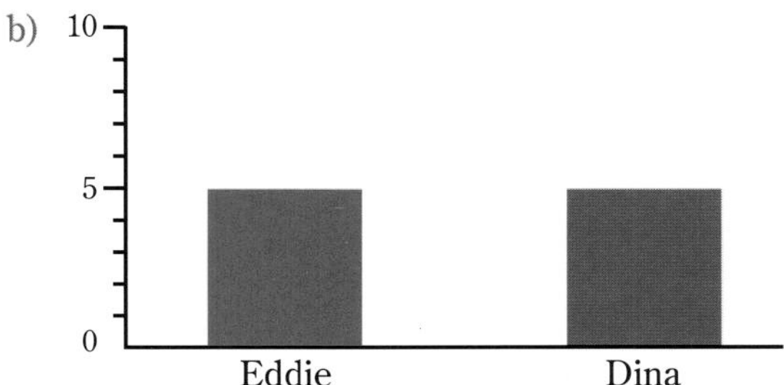

Eddie, Dina: equal power. A sort of mini-sparring match, nobody wins.

c) 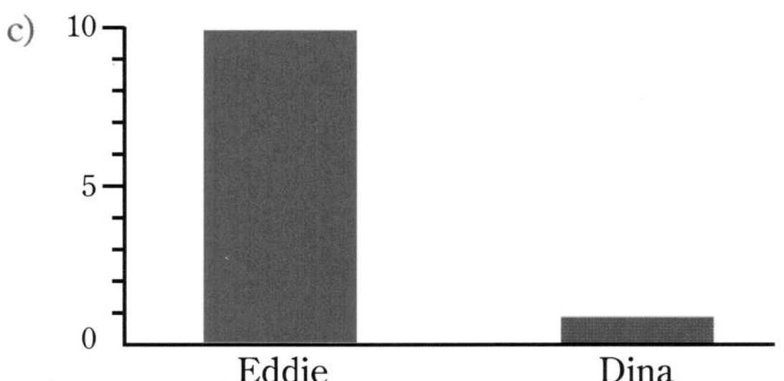

Dina: low status. Guilty, genuinely sorry, afraid of Eddie.

Eddie, Dina: equal power. A sort of mini-sparring match, nobody wins.

3 Now apply some of these ideas to this longer extract below practising the whole scene in pairs.

Bruises by Judy Upton

Kate has left college and come down to Worthing to look for her mum, Myrtle, and has tracked her down.

Kate joins Myrtle. They move to the chairs and tables.

Myrtle: I hope it's defrosted properly. I've only just come back from Tesco's. I wasn't going to start on it till this evening. I'd have bought a bigger one if you'd written to let me know you were coming....'scuse fingers.

She dollops a huge lump of gâteau onto a plate, hands it to ***Kate****.*

Have some extra cherries.

She takes out a little plastic pot of glacé cherries, tips some on ***Kate's*** *plate.*

They never put enough in, do they? So how's college?

Kate: Why didn't you call me?

Myrtle: They cut off the phone.

Kate: Is... I mean are you still living with... ?

Myrtle: He's good for me. He makes me smile. I painted him, do you want to see? He said to never show anyone but...

Kate: Then don't show me. I can't eat this. I'm sorry.

Myrtle: Shall I make you something else? Salad? Something healthy? Have you gone vegetarian?

Kate: Mum... I don't think I'll go back after the holidays. I don't fit in, I don't understand half the stuff they're trying to teach me, or why I should need to know those things. I thought I might try to get a job down here or something, so we could see each other sometimes...

Myrtle: How's Mel?

Kate: Dad's fine.

Myrtle: I miss him.

Kate: So why...

Myrtle: I wish we were still friends.

Kate: You can't be friends and love someone.

Myrtle: Is this from experience, love?

Kate: It's something I've been thinking about.

Myrtle: Andy?

Kate: He's my best friend, always will be… and no, no, I *do* love him, but it's not like when you meet someone and you feel…

Myrtle: That's exactly it. How it was with Duncan. I met him and I felt –

Kate: I don't want to hear about Duncan!

Myrtle: I was talking about *me*, my feelings.

Kate: I hate Duncan.

Myrtle: Kate, love, don't –

Kate: I hate the way he treats you – it's all phoney, he's completely phoney – that's why I'm not going back to college.

Myrtle: I don't see how Duncan –

Kate: Don't you see! Everyone there, they're all like him!

Play the scene in pairs, but focus in particular on the status and motives of the characters. Consider:

- Who is vulnerable?
- Who 'controls' where the conversation is going?
- What does each character want? Is it simply to be listened to?

As you play it, think about how small gestures and movements can convey the status or power within the conversation. What might be the effect of Myrtle placing her hand on her daughter's arm at one point? Would Kate sit or stand?

Commentary

Write about your performance and comment on your decisions and the status and motives of the characters in this scene. Alternatively, write about any other scene you are working on.

Six final exercises

1 Private preparation

Every character you play has a private life, or a history before the play begins, even if it is never seen on stage.

Imagine your character in his or her 'private space', perhaps in their bedroom or on a beach – anywhere. Mime their actions and what they pick up, how they hold things, how they sit down, how they move, etc.

2 Collage

Trawl through magazines, or the props cupboard. Find any number of things that will help build a picture of your character. Imagine you are playing Romeo, for example. You might look for:

We'll call him Romeo. Such a handsome, gentle-looking boy.

- photos or artwork of people who are like this character, or have aspects of this character (they could be photos of animals, creatures, etc.)
- objects or items that represent the character, or that the character might like.

One line, one phrase

3 Whether your character speaks or not, find or invent the one line or phrase that best sums them up. It might be a sound, a laugh, a short word. Once you have decided on it, take the 'phrase' for a walk around the room and practise saying it until you are comfortable with it. For example, 'All you need is love'.

4 Pair confidential

With a partner, talk about events or emotions in the play or piece of drama. Your partner should say nothing other than "I see", or "Right". This should not be scripted, but done in an informal, conversational way.

It just happened. We were at the ball, and for a moment I took off my mask, and there she was. It hit me right between the eyes, her beauty… and I knew she was the one.

1 2 3 4 5 6 7 8 9 10

5 Biography

Tell a partner your character's life story, either real (i.e., based on information given in the play or known by you) or invented. Allow your partner to stop you and ask questions for more detail or clarification.

Of course, my parents brought me up to run the household, take over the family. And there was always this hate of the Capulets. If we broke a glass, or ripped some fine cloth, we'd curse and say, "That's the work of the Capulets!"

6 Hot-seating

This is a well-known technique which is very useful in explaining actions and behaviour. The interrogators will need to be well-prepared and know your character well so they can fire questions at you about your role in the drama. You answer in role, as the character.

So, you were just flirting with Rosaline, were you, Romeo?

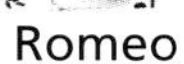

Romeo

Juliet

Mercutio

7 Devised Work

In this chapter you will:

- *discover ways to develop ideas from source material*
- *learn how to hone ideas through development and negotiation.*

Working from sources

In most syllabuses, you will be expected to do work that arises not directly from one written script, but from one or more other sources. Sometimes it is helpful if these sources have some sort of common link to begin with; on other occasions, a random selection can spark interesting ideas.

The single source

The single source could be anything:

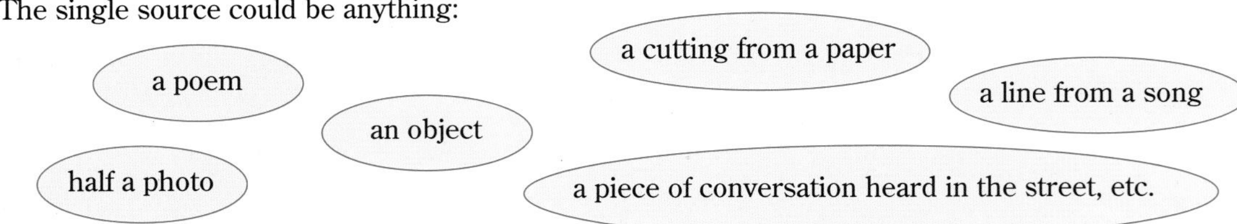

However, for the purposes of this work, let's start with an image. In groups, look at this picture.

Vendedor de Agua y Limon, Lorenzo Tiepolo

1 In your group, discuss:

- What is happening in the picture? Who appear to be the key figures?
- Who are in the background and what are they doing?
- What significance do the items of clothing and objects have? What are they? What are they for?

Further discussion

Focus on detail:

The woman on the left has her hand on the man's arm. Is this a touch of intimacy or rejection, or perhaps both?

Although the man holding the drink is quite central, it is towards the other man, with the round object on his back, to whom she looks. Why?

Possibilities

2 Now work on your own. Choose one of the following as a way of taking the source material a stage further towards performance.

A number of possibilities arise from the picture:

a. A straight narrative – there appears to be a story here. Where does it start and how does it end? Spend two minutes only rapidly brainstorming in writing one possible version. Give the characters names and give details of what happens.

b. A theme or issue might be taken up and developed – 'the power of persuasion' or 'a strong woman'. Spend two minutes only listing possible thematic titles (however tenuous) for the image by adding to these:

- secrecy
- knowledge.

Now return to your group and share your stories for the painting first. Then share your thematic titles.

3 For the moment, discard the stories but choose one of the thematic titles given to the painting. As a group, discuss and note down (you will all need to keep notes for your working notebook or commentary file) details about how this might be developed by bringing in other sources, such as songs and poems, and how your group might build on this image to create a collage of new images or performances.

Commentary

Write up your ideas.

Stuck for ideas?

4 If you are having trouble thinking of making links between the image and other sources, try the following:

1. Start with a frozen tableau of the picture, with the group taking up the roles in the painting.

↓

2. Follow the woman's 'path in life', as she has to confront an issue or problem (this is where you could bring in one of your earlier stories).

↓

3. Introduce a dance to a suitable piece of music at a moment of strife or despair.

↓

4. Finish with her safe and well, with the reading of a suitable extract or poem.

↓

END

Exploration

Organic work

It is best to work organically – that is to say, to experiment with some different ideas and let the work flow out of practical moulding. Start with a few ideas, such as a simple mime or the tableau suggested above (nothing too ambitious), and then let the drama or collage grow from there.

Idea
Exchange/explore

Take forward

Commentary

Keep notes throughout under the following headings:

Initial thoughts:

- where we started: looking at the image
- first impressions and ideas

Further exploration, discussion and negotiation:

- first practical work and movement ideas, etc.
- other possible materials brought in

What we decided – what we set out to achieve:

- how we shaped our ideas
- what my role was.
- how I shaped and developed my role or roles. What were the physical and vocal skills required?

Here is the beginning of one student's commentary or evaluation of her work (extract):

> We were given a still from an X-Files episode. The image was a very dark monochrome one, with Mulder's face in shadow, in a laboratory.
>
> My first thought, which I shared with my group, was that Mulder had a 'dark side'. We spent some time discussing the series, which was fun, but didn't lead us anywhere, and we were running out of ideas a bit, when David suggested we took up the pose of Mulder over the lab table in the picture. We did this, and it looked really strange – these two boys and two girls, all with this grim look, in a line. But there was something good about it. Gita said we looked like a production line, but not a real one – more like one from another world. We wondered what the people on the production line could be dealing with. Someone else said 'the dead'!
>
> Gita's really good at art, so she said she'd draw a picture of what one of these workers might look like. I said we should remember Mulder's dark side – so she drew a sketch of a character like this…
>
> We weren't sure where to go next, so we showed our drama teacher our Mulder pose, in a line, with some basic movements we'd added – like robots. We spaced ourselves out equally, to make us look less individual. Our teacher said she was reminded of a line by a poet called T S Eliot 'We are the hollow men'. We decided to use this line, and others from the poem.

Multiple sources

Another way to start is by gathering together a number of linked or randomly selected resources and using them as a way of stimulating ideas. In this case, the starting point was 'gold'. The following were quickly gathered together knowing this simple link. Look at them and then use the chart below to start developing ideas.

Nothing gold can stay

Nature's first green is gold
Her hardest hue to hold
Her early leaf's a flower
But only so an hour
Then leaf subsides to leaf
So Eden sank to grief
So dawn goes down today
Nothing gold can stay

Robert Frost

Gold! Always believe in your soul
You've got the power to know
You're indestructible...

(1980s pop song by Spandau Ballet)

All that glisters is not gold ...

Shakespeare's *Merchant of Venice*

1 Copy and complete these charts on your own.

Similarities

Poem	Pop song	Mask	Shakespeare
Talks about things not lasting, about gold disappearing – negative feel.		Hides things?	Says you can't judge something, even gold, by its appearance – also negative.

Differences

	Positive – says person is indestructible		

Exploring ideas

What does 'gold' suggest to you – a priceless statue, like the one opposite?

2 Now read the following, then, in a group, discuss and add any of your own ideas.

Possibilities

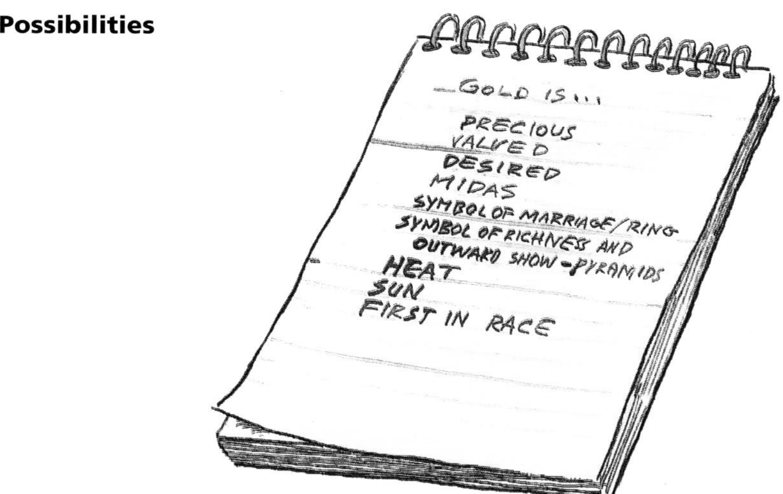

Group activities

Follow this process as a way of exploring the theme of 'gold'.

1 **Warm-up**

Sit in a circle with the rest of the group. Pass an imagined gold bar around the circle. On the first 'pass round', the group should show their extreme desire and love for the gold by their actions and facial expressions. You may add words if you wish, or keep the piece a mime.

On the second 'pass round', your expressions and gestures turn to disgust and hatred, as if the gold bar were the worst sort of poisoned or infected substance.

Now, in turn, hold the gold bar in front of you, as it is passed round for the third time. Describe what you see inside it, what images are reflected, what thoughts come to your mind. These could be positive, or could reflect the disgust of the second 'pass round'.

Short scenes

2 Now prepare and present these two short scenes arising from the theme 'gold'. Both have been started for you, but your group will need to take them forward …

1)

Vicar:	With this ring I thee wed.
Groom:	With this ring I thee wed.
Bride:	With that ring? You must be joking!
Groom:	What's the matter with it?
Bride:	Matter? It's not gold … that's the 'matter'!

... now you continue.

2)

Wife:	Midas – where are you?
(*Enters*)	
Midas:	Don't come close … don't touch me!
Wife:	My dear, what on earth's … (*Screams*)
Midas:	Stop! Stay still!
Wife:	It's moving! The floor's moving!
Midas:	It's not moving … it's the gold. It's creeping, like a disease. Get out!
Wife:	I can't; it's so … beautiful.
Midas:	It's not. It's ugly … rotten to the core… you must leave!
Wife:	Look at it … feel it … it's warm on my legs … my arms … my mouth … the taste is …
Midas:	Darling! (*She is frozen to the spot*)

... now you continue.

Moving the idea into a rhythm

3 To finish the sequence, as a group or class try chanting this simple rhyme, increasing in speed and volume as you do so until you reach the last syllable which should be shouted out in unison.

Build into it some simple choreographed moves.

gold gold gold
gold gold gold
mine mine mine
mine mine mine

hold hold hold
hold hold hold
mine mine mine
mine mine mine

gold gold gold
gold gold gold
yours yours yours
yours yours yours

hold hold hold
hold hold hold
gold gold gold
gold gold gold

mine yours
yours mine
mine yours
yours mine

hold gold
gold hold
hold hold
hold HOLD
HOLD HOLD
GOLD GOLD
GOLD GOLD
GOLD GOLD

GOLD!!!

Presentation

4 Perform the collage of pieces. Start with your circle improvisation, moving into the two short dramas, and ending with the verse-dance.

Commentary

When you have finished, write about how well the 'collage' of devised pieces worked. Were you able to link them together in any way?

8 Spontaneous Improvisation

In this chapter you will:

- *look at the key skills involved*
- *put those skills into practice.*

What's the point?

Whilst not all exam boards mention the option of 'spontaneous improvisation' by name, it is worth exploring the possibilities it brings in developing drama, and as an end in itself.

In the most simple form, spontaneous improvisation can be used for warming-up before other work. At its most sophisticated level, it involves quick mental thought, a strong grasp of performance skills, and a real sense of what the rest of your group are doing. It also assists exploration of role in scripted work.

What is it?

A general definition would be that it is a piece of drama resulting from a stimulus, such as a photo, a phrase or short poem, which is performed by a student or group of students without any real time for thought or reflection.

Here are some comments from teachers and students who have watched such improvisations:

> It's easy to do badly, difficult to do well.

> We don't treat it like real drama – it's really just playing.

> Usually our spontaneous improvisations end up being funny – even when we don't intend them to.

> They always seem to fall apart at the end – or our teacher has to stop them from going on and on.

How good are you? Perhaps you have mastered the skills already?

1 2 3 4 5 6 7 8 9 10

1 Starting off in a small group, try this improvisation. Keep to these rules:

- **no discussion** of the possibilities
- a **time limit** of two minutes
- must be '**serious**'
- **no props** other than a chair or two.

The stimulus is the phrase:

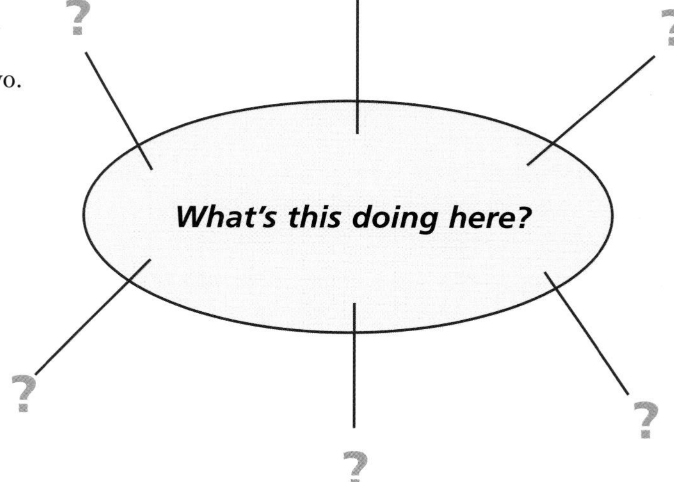

Commentary

When you have finished, discuss these points briefly in your groups:

- How easy was it to begin?
- Who started the 'ball rolling'?
- How did you feel about their choice?
- Did the drama change direction at any point (did the story develop significantly)?
- Did anyone do anything that made it difficult for the rest?
- How successfully did it end?

An example

2 Now read this example of one group's beginning of such an improvisation. In it there is some indication of the actions. Three students, A, B and C, are taking part.

A:	(*Stooping to look at something*) What's this doing here?
B:	It's mine.
A:	(*Slightly surprised*) Yours?
B:	Yes. I... err... bought it.
A:	What? You know we can't afford it. (*Getting cross*)
C:	Yes, we can, I won some money on a lottery ticket today.
A:	That was lucky – can I have some money?
C:	You can all have some.

Look at student C's contribution. In pairs, discuss in what way this was unhelpful to the improvisation.

This is sometimes called 'blocking', as in 'blocking the development of the drama'.

There are all sorts of ways the first four lines could be developed – but in particular the conflict between A and B is established and can be taken forward.

3 Ask two of your group to run the first four lines in your group, trying to keep the conflict going. If a third character enters, they should either:

- increase the conflict
- or, if they are to play peacemaker, help develop the story.

More about blocking

Blocking happens in several situations:

A) When someone in the drama introduces a new piece of information which is not apparently linked to the developing story. This is best avoided: it can be managed by a very quick-thinking group, but more often than not, it kills the development.

Example:

A character announces she is pregnant when the drama is about the imminent building of a new bypass. This would be fine IF the character is the main protestor and she had aimed to lie in front of the bulldozers, but not helpful if only indirectly related to the main storyline.

B) When a performer doesn't allow the development of the story by 'blocking' another performer's idea, often so they can develop their own.

Example:

A:	What's this doing here?
B:	I put it there… it's for you – something special for our anniversary – it's been five years since that moment… you know, the one…
A:	It's not our anniversary – oh, I know what this is, I bought it today…

This can also work, if the second idea is good, and A doesn't mind having his or her idea hijacked, but sensitivity is needed.

Dominating the improvisation

One common problem is that often one or two students can end up dominating the improvisation. Alternatively, everyone speaks at once and the drama gets swamped by conversation.

4 Try this short improvisation, again based on a phrase. The rules are the same as before with these added ones:

- No one must speak while someone else is speaking.
- Each member of the group must speak *in order** (decide numbers beforehand so that A speaks first, B second, and so on. Groups must be no more than 5).

* This is good practice for avoiding the problems above. Of course, in the 'real thing' there is no need to do this.

Stimulus: *A Birthday Surprise.*

Commentary

Discuss how easy it was to keep to the rules. Who was struggling?

Key Pointer!

When performing such an instant improvisation:

- Allow one member of the group to establish the action or story. Don't rush in straightaway.
- Generally, don't speak when others are speaking.
- Don't race your words; keep them simple and to the point.
- Don't make your story or response over-complicated.

9 Applying Dramatic Styles and Forms

In this chapter you will:

- *explore the notion of 'genre' and 'convention'*
- *look at a well-known dramatic form and apply it to your own work.*

Much of the work you do proceeds from script-based work, but in the development of your own work it can be useful and interesting to apply some specific forms of theatre that have had an impact on theatre.

Genres

Take a simple story:

A young woman abandons her child. Some time later, the woman's husband disappears.
Years pass. She thinks he is dead. She falls in love and remarries.
Her husband returns and ... ?

1 In groups, discuss the different ways this would be presented if it was:

- a UK-based soap opera
- an X-Files story
- a 19th century costume drama.

2 Look at this genre chart. You may have done something similar as part of English or Media Studies lessons. Can you recognise which one of the three genres above it is?

Now copy the chart and complete it for the others.

Settings	Typical character/s	Object/icons	Language
Government Office Laboratory	Lab technician Shadowy older man	Scalpel Plastic gloves	There's no logical explanation. You don't really believe that.

Convention

One of the key conventions of this sort of drama is that, at the end, the seemingly logical explanation is challenged by some mysterious final event that cannot be explained rationally. All genres have such conventions, as you will see later in the chapter.

Applying the genre

3 When you have finished completing the chart, take one simple scene – the wife finding out about her husband's disappearance – and select one of the genres above.

Before you work on it, decide in your group:

- where the scene will take place
- what the wife does or is (for example, a job, her age, etc.)
- who will tell her
- what sorts of things will be said.

Now improvise the scene on the basis above. When you have worked it up into something that is not too long (perhaps 3–5 minutes maximum), present it to the rest of the class. Are they able to tell which genre it belongs to?

Or did the presentation slip into 'spoof'? This happens when:

- the drama is intentionally, or unintentionally, funny
- the characters are very exaggerated and almost like caricatures
- the plot is very predictable.

How can you make it work as drama?

4
- Practise the activity above again, but this time downplay the language somewhat.
- Make it less obviously part of that genre, or change one element, perhaps setting it somewhere unusual or playing it very seriously and not for laughs.
- Make the emotions genuine and not an imitation of what you have seen elsewhere.
- Develop the drama and finish the whole story.

Commentary

Write about the piece. What elements of the genre did you include? Which did you change, or drop altogether? Were you able to produce a drama that worked as drama, not as a spoof on the original genre?

8
9
10

Drama form: Greek tragedy and the chorus

The story at the start of this chapter is essentially an old one. It is related, at least in part, to the myth of Oedipus, and was told by one of the first great playwrights, Sophocles', in his play *Oedipus the King*.

Read this version of the story.

Oedipus' daughter Antigone in a production by the RSC

Oedipus the King by Sophocles

Oedipus is the wise and well-liked ruler of Thebes. But he mistakenly believes he is the son of King Polybus of Corinth and his queen. He became the ruler of Thebes because he rescued the city from the Sphinx, a female monster that had terrorised the city by devouring its citizens when they failed to solve the riddle it set. He was given the city's widowed queen, Jocasta, as a reward. Oedipus left Corinth forever because it had been prophesied that he would kill his father and marry his mother. While on the way to Thebes, Oedipus met an old man with five servants. Oedipus argued with him and, losing his temper, killed the old man and four of his servants.

Despite Oedipus' popularity, Thebes is suffering a terrible plague. Oedipus consults the Delphic oracle – a woman with divine powers who communicates the words of the gods. She tells him that the plague will end only when the murderer of Jocasta's first husband, King Laius, has been found and punished. Oedipus resolves to find Laius' killer, but as he conducts the investigation, it becomes apparent that his own past is being uncovered. He starts to suspect that the old man he killed on his way to Thebes was Laius. In the end, Oedipus learns that he himself was abandoned to die as a baby by Laius and Jocasta many years before. They had feared a prophecy that said their baby son would kill his father, and marry his mother. He finds out that he survived and was adopted by the ruler of Corinth. He also learns that as a grown man he has unwittingly fulfilled the Delphic oracle's prophecy – he has indeed killed his real father, and wedded his own mother.

Jocasta hangs herself on learning the facts about her husband and son. Oedipus then blinds himself with needles. Alone, he can no longer see the world around him but at last knows the awful truth of his own life.

The chorus and tragedy

The chorus

Sophocles was just one of many Greek dramatists who developed drama out of the rituals of song and dance, over 400 years before the birth of Christ. Central to their work was the notion of a chorus. This varied according to the dramatist.

The chorus may originally have been dancers at a religious festival who began to speak with the priest. When a second speaker was added, the beginnings of 'play' as we know it started, with the chorus or dancers, sometimes up to 50 in number, and the two 'actors'.

This was later reduced to 12 performers who were now doing much more than singing and, although Sophocles added three more to make 15, he also added a third 'actor'.

The Masked Ball

While these main tragic actors showed the extremes man and woman could suffer, the chorus expressed the views and feelings – and the judgement – of the ordinary people.

Later, in Elizabethan drama, the name 'chorus' came to represent a single person, often the actor who spoke the prologue and epilogue, as in Shakespeare's *Romeo and Juliet.*

Commentary

Discuss any characters who you think act as a form of chorus in any television programmes, films or plays you have seen. Think in particular of those who rarely, if ever, have stories of their own, but seem to comment on other people's lives.

Reread the Oedipus story. Which characters, or groups, would the chorus have represented in Sophocles' story?

The conventions of tragedy

Sophocles' notion of tragedy came to have great influence on drama over the centuries and can be seen even today in the work of playwrights like Arthur Miller.

This notion of tragedy, shared with many other Greek dramatists, often centred around:

- an important (but understandable) person brought down by a weakness or flaw that may or may not be his or her fault
- a tragic error – a moment when the hero makes the fatal mistake that will lead to his downfall
- signs and omens of this fall, which the hero fails to, or only partly recognises
- strong emotions, and the hero torn between good and evil (sometimes unwittingly, as in Oedipus' case)
- usually a tragic dénouement or climax, in which the hero comes to see his or her fault
- questions about whether people can control their own fate, or whether their lives are pre-determined (already decided by god or gods).

Commentary

Look at the story of Oedipus. Make notes which show how each of the above is true of his tragedy. For example, what is his first, and perhaps most important, 'fatal error'?

Also, write briefly about any current stories on television, in films, or in plays that follow the same sort of pattern. Are there any significant differences, other than modern speech?

Applying the form

So, what is the point of using or taking any of these ideas for your own work?

Firstly, the stories the Greek dramatists told can be considered universal. Whilst it is highly unlikely that someone will kill his father and marry his mother, the idea of a great or well-regarded person whose weakness brings him down is common.

Also, as you have seen, whilst the traditional chorus is rare in contemporary drama, the person who comments on the action does exist, and the idea of a narrator – even a 'voice-over' – who can step back and view the action is still used.

Inventing a chorus

1 Take any well-known television soap opera, or other television drama you know. Although there are characters who comment on the action in these programmes, they often differ in that they, too, have stories weaved around them – and for a few weeks they become the protagonists.

2 Invent two new characters, using the pictures below, if you wish. They can either have names, or simply be 'young hairdresser', 'man who works at farm', etc.

Chorus 1

Chorus 2

3 Write or improvise a short monologue in which they comment on goings-on in the story. Remember:
- Their comments must reflect the ordinary person or viewers' attitudes.
- They must not, themselves, be directly involved in the action.

If this works, create a larger group. Can you create a similar dialogue for four or five people in the story? In other words, can you create a Greek-style chorus?

Devised work

4 Now devise your own story as a group. It should have a modern setting, but also have many of the features of classical Greek tragedy. You will need to have:

- a tragic hero
- the hero's weakness or fault (pride, greed, ambition, etc.)
- a key error he or she makes
- clues or omens in the story, some of which the audience know but the hero doesn't (dramatic irony), all of which are finally revealed to the hero
- a powerful climax or end when the hero is brought down.

Using the idea of a Chorus

5 Within your drama, bring in a chorus. You can base it on ideas you used earlier, but remember that the chorus can be either:

a conventional chorus which comments on the story and judges the main actors, but which doesn't take part

or…

a more modern chorus which takes part in the story, but acts as a confidant for the audience, telling them what is happening.

The language of the chorus can be:

natural and part of the normal action

or…

more stylised, with chants, songs or verses, like the original chorus.

Would a modern chorus look like this?

Commentary

You will have quite a few notes from your earlier work. Now write up a full report of your work on the drama form of the Greek Tragedy.

Make sure you include:

- Initial notes on what 'genre' is (remember the *X-Files* chart on page 98).

Start:

> *In our work on Greek tragedy, we first of all looked at what 'genre' is. The genre of a piece of work is...*

- A brief explanation of the key elements of Greek tragedy, the tragic hero and the chorus.

Start:

> *The 'genre' or form 'Greek tragedy' began many years ago, well before the birth of Christ. The main elements in the tragic form were...*

- How the form is still relevant today.

Start:

> *Although the tragic form is centuries old, the same sorts of stories exist today. For example...*

- How you applied the tragic form and idea of the chorus to your own work.

Start:

> *Our group devised a way of using the tragic form, and the chorus. It was as follows. First we...*

- Conclude with a general comment about the Greek dramatic form and how well it worked. What benefits, if any, did it bring to your dramatic work?

10 Exploring Texts for Performance

In this chapter you will:

- *look at the possibilities a text offers for performance*
- *explore how to 'action' the words*
- *finalise a style and interpretation for a performance.*

A script on the page, even if it is of a play you have seen before, can seem a flat, lifeless thing. Even if you then read it carefully, trying to see the words become action can be daunting for a performer, like speaking a foreign language for the first time.

Bringing a drama to life

However, a whole range of practitioners – directors, actors, choreographers – have developed hundreds of ways of breathing life into a piece of written drama. In this chapter, you will deal with a few of them, and will develop some of your own.

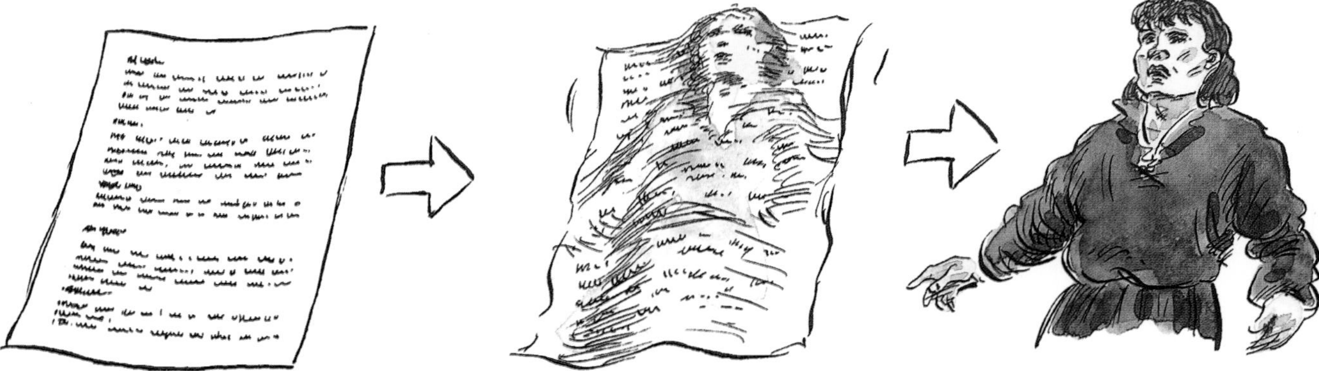

The work will take you through a number of exercises and stages. For your own benefit, and as a way of remembering the process when you are working on your own scripts, this process has been split into a number of stages:

Stage 1: The Comfort Zone Knowing the narrative Warm-ups Reading the text 'Actioning' the language	Stage 3: Telling the story Pair statues with themes Group statues with themes Adding words to actions
Stage 2: Initial thoughts Exploring the background Powerful words, powerful lines What's going on?	Stage 4: Focused work and performance Working in pairs Physical work Breaking down the scene Final report

Stage 1: The Comfort Zone

Whatever script you are dealing with, it helps if you are thoroughly comfortable with the main elements of the story, regardless of whether you understand the characters or why they behave as they do. For the purposes of this work, we are going to look at Shakespeare's *The Tempest*.

Knowing the narrative

There are many ways of getting to know the story of a play. Reading it through is essential, but often there are helpful summaries within the introduction, or elsewhere in the script.

Here is a basic summary of the story of *The Tempest*.

The play begins with a storm conjured by Prospero, who years earlier, as the rightful duke of Milan, had been set adrift with his daughter Miranda by his usurping brother, Antonio. Shipwrecked on a magical island, Prospero learned the art of magic and set free a sprite named Ariel – who had been tormented by the sorceress Sycorax. Sycorax's son Caliban has become Prospero's slave. Prospero now raises the tempest to trap Antonio and his courtiers, casting them on the shores of his island at the opening of the play.

Although Ariel brings all the ship's company to shore, Ferdinand, son of Alonso, the king of Naples, is separated from the others and is believed drowned. Ariel helps prevent plots against Prospero by Caliban and against Alonso by Antonio. Ariel then appears to Alonso and Antonio as a harpy and reproaches them for their treatment of Prospero. Alonso, believing Ferdinand dead, is certain that his son's death was punishment for his own crime and has a change of heart. In fact, Ferdinand has been brought alive to Prospero and has fallen in love with Miranda, his daughter. Prospero, persuaded that Antonio and company are repentant, brings everyone together and prepares to return to Milan to reclaim his throne.

Warm-ups

Warm-up 1: Master and slave

It is not vital for the warm-up to be related to the story, but it can help.

In pairs, one of you sit on a chair (the master) and give orders to the other (the slave). These can range from the mundane, "Get me my slippers" to the obscure, "The police are at the door, cover for me". The master should increase the rate at which the orders come so that the slave/servant's job becomes increasingly difficult.

Then swap roles.

Finally, try the scenario in which the slave determines the situation, appearing unrequested with items to drink, or papers to sign, until the master is as much slave as his or her servant.

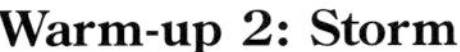

Warm-up 2: Storm

Form a still tableau in this way:

1. As a group, stand in a triangle formation.
2. The person facing foremost should assume the position of steering the ship's enormous wheel.
3. The others hold ropes, or climb masts.
4. As a group, count down in unison, "Five, four, three, two, one" and then fall to the floor, as if a wave has knocked you flat.
5. Count, "One, two, three, four, five" in unison and change positions so whoever is hauling the ropes now steers the ship, and so on.
6. Count, "Five, four, three, two, one" and fall to the floor once again.
7. Count, "One, two, three, four, five" and assume new positions.

END

Reading the text

The following extract from *The Tempest* features Prospero and Caliban.

Prospero: Thou poisonous slave, got by the devil himself.
Upon thy wicked dam, come forth!

Enter Caliban

Caliban: As wicked dew as e'er my mother brush'd
With raven's feather from unwholesome fen
Drop on you both! a south-west blow on ye,
And blister you all o'er.

Prospero: For this, be sure, to-night thou shalt have cramps,
Side-stitches that shall pen thy breath up; urchins
Shall, for that vast of night that they may work,
All exercise on thee; thou shalt be pinch'd
As thick as honey-combs, each pinch more stinging
Than bees that made them.

Caliban: I must eat my dinner.
This island's mine, by Sycorax my mother,
Which thou tak'st from me. When thou camest first,
Thou strok'dst me, and mad'st much of me; wouldst give me
Water with berries in't; and teach me how
To name the bigger light, and how the less,
That burn by day and night; and then I lov'd thee
And shew'd thee all the qualities of the isle,
The fresh springs, brine pits, barren place, and fertile;
Cursed be I that did so! - All the charms
Of Sycorax, toads, beetles, bats, light on you!
For I am all the subjects that you have,
Which first was mine own king; and here you sty me
In this hard rock, whiles you do keep from me
The rest of the island.

Prospero: Thou most lying slave,
Whom stripes may move, not kindness: I have used thee
Filth as thou art, with human care; and lodged thee
In mine own cell, till thou didst seek to violate
The honour of my child.

* stripes - blows/whippings

'Actioning' the language

It is a particular problem of Shakespeare that the language can be difficult to grasp on first reading. This can be true of more recent texts, too. Here are a number of exercises to make you feel more comfortable with it.

Take the text for a walk

1 Move round the studio or room reading the lines out loud to yourself – not trying to act them but simply reading. Don't worry about accurate pronunciation.

2 Now repeat the exercise. This time, change direction every time you meet any form of punctuation.

3 Finally, say each line to a different wall in the room, saying nothing as you move between each one.

4 Do these exercises as many times as you need to, until you feel relatively comfortable with the feel of the words, even if you don't understand them all.

Commentary

Think about:

- how helpful the exercises were in getting over the barrier of the language
- whether you can think of any exercises of your own, also involving movements (but not 'acting'), which you could use to 'free up' the words on the page. For example, working in pairs playing verbal tennis, with one of you saying a few words and the other 'sending back' the last word spoken.

Exploring the background

It is not always necessary to know the background to a play – about the writer or the time he or she lived in – but it can lead to fresh ideas for the performer or director. Here are three things that could be called 'background' to *The Tempest.*

- Shakespeare lived in a time of political upheaval. Queen Elizabeth I and then King James both had to repress rebellion, and civil war was always a possibility.
- Exploration, discovery of new places and peoples ('The New World' of America, for example) had captured the public imagination.
- People were still incredibly superstitious and many would readily believe in magic and the power of other forces.

1 Discuss, in your groups, to what extent any of these themes is reflected in the words said by Caliban and Prospero, or by the story as a whole. Reread the summary on page 107, if you need to.

Powerful words, powerful lines

2 Now, on your own, go through the scene on page 109, and pick out two or three lines or phrases that you see as particularly powerful or important. Say them out loud several times before sharing them with your group.

At this stage, there is no need to say why you chose them.

What's going on?

3 Now, as a group, say what you think is happening in this scene. Consider:

- What has happened before?
- What the subject of the conversation is?
- What might happen as a result (of course, you know from the summary of the play, but is there *evidence* that this is going to happen?).

Commentary

Write a detailed commentary on what you think this short extract from the play is about, mentioning key words and phrases and including any discussions from your group.

Telling the story

You have begun to give the language and the scene life by sounding out some lines, walking with the text and discussing the action of the scene. Now it is time to do some more physical work exploring some themes that might arise from the play.

These are all exercises involving statue work.

1 2 3 4 5

1 In pairs:
Create a series of statues representing:

Slave	Anger	Power	Hatred
Love	Island	Freedom	

2 In groups:
Create a series of group statues representing:

Love	Slave	Island
Magic	Freedom	Revenge

These can be reordered and played with either on your own control with your group deciding when to change from one statue to the next, or on your teacher's word. If working well, the 'statues' should be able to merge into each other so that they become almost one continuous piece of movement work.

3 Adding words from the extract:

A further exploration can be to add a few key lines or phrases, perhaps the ones you selected earlier, which can either be spoken by the members of the group as they move into statues, or by an outside narrator. For example:

Line/phrase	Statue
Thou strok'dst me	Love
Poisonous slave	Slave
This island's mine	Island
Wicked dew	Magic
The bigger light	Freedom
Curs'd be I	Revenge

Focused work and performance

4 Ask questions about what sort of creature Caliban is.

• What sort of monster is he?	–	Is he stupid? Dumb? Violent? Untrustworthy?
• How does he look?	–	Is he hunch-backed? Creepy? Tall and willowy? Small and plump, like a toad?

5 What about Prospero? He was the Duke of Milan, but he's been on the island for many years.

• What sort of 'creature' is Prospero?		
• What sort of 'master'?	–	Is he intelligent? A genius? Violent or peaceful? Respected? Feared?
How does he look?	–	Is he tall and forceful? Slight and bookish? Large and swarthy, like an Italian gangster?

There are no correct answers, but you have to find your own way through.

Working on the scene in pairs

You have done a lot of movement and space work, so ideas for where to stand, how to use seating (for example, a chair), the floor space, and so on, should be familiar to you.

6 First, adopt an 'attitude' for each character. For example:

Prospero:	angry, but also disappointed with Caliban's ungratefulness
Caliban:	resentful, half-afraid, but defiant

7 Play the scene on page 109 again, and include these features:
- a moment when Caliban almost breaks into tears
- a moment when Caliban's words sound almost beautiful
- a moment when Prospero roughly handles Caliban.

Commentary

Discuss with your partner how well this version worked. What needs changing?

Go back to the text and look at it together. Have you identified and used key lines and changes of mood in the speeches? For example, Caliban makes several references to nature ('the bigger light', 'berries' and 'fresh springs'). What does this suggest about his 'nature' or his character? Does he sound like a monster?

Physical work

8 Spend some time working on the physical aspect of the scene. Talk and work on how the two characters move. For example, are Prospero's gestures quick, or slow and deliberate? How does Caliban move? Does he creep? Slither? Stride bow-legged like a fat dwarf?

Breaking down the scene

9 Look at the text carefully, identifying the changing tempo and mood and the positioning of the characters. Is Prospero centre stage when he calls Caliban to 'come forth'? Where does Caliban come from? Does he approach Prospero or stay still in one corner?

Make your own decisions, both for the part you are playing and your partner's, with regard to how you speak:

- Do you lose your temper?
- Do you shout?
- Would quiet words work at any point?
- Is there resentment in your voice?
- Do you interrupt each other?
- Are there pauses in the lines, when you move or make a gesture?
- Who is in control in this scene? Who has the 'status'? Does it change?
- What is your motive? What do you want – to be liked? To be respected?

10 Play the scene through, trying out different moves, moods, uses of pace and characteristics. Make your own decisions and arrive at an agreed performance before showing it to the rest of the class.

Watch the other pairs and try to analyse the different interpretations. Which works best of the ones you watch? Keep notes as you go.

Commentary

Write up a full report of your work on *The Tempest*, including, in particular, notes on how you came to decide on your final interpretation of the scene between Caliban and Prospero.

- **Be very specific in your comments. Refer directly to lines in the scene, and how you played them.**

NOT

We played the scene like a servant and master.

BUT

When I say, "Come forth" I mean it as an order – there is no gentleness in my voice.

- **Mention your reasoning for movements, gestures and other performance decisions.**

NOT

We played the scene quickly; that seemed to work.

BUT

On the line, "This island's mine" I wanted Caliban to interrupt Prospero, as if he couldn't hold his resentment in any more.

- **Finish by saying how successful, or otherwise, your version was, with reasons!**

NOT

Our scene worked okay, after all, everybody said we did well.

BUT

I thought the interplay between us was really good, like these two people were really close, even though they also hated each other. I thought we brought that out in the odd moment of tenderness, followed by violence.

A full-length script: *Watching Brief*

The following short play has been provided by the author for you to work from. It is not suggested that this is better or more appropriate than texts that have been selected by your teacher, but it does offer certain opportunities you may find helpful:

- at least four main speaking roles (possibly five, although 'Voice' can be shared between the other characters, if you wish)
- substantial 'chunks' of speaking with some reasonable monologues, and also a good deal of one-line interplay.
- no in-depth description of scene, or set, which offers opportunities both for detailed design and lighting, or a sparse, minimalist approach. You may also like to consider possibilities for mask or puppetry work.

Without saying too much about the text, it may be worth pointing out that previous productions have dealt with the issue of 'the body' in different ways. In one production, there was no box, no body. Instead, it was as if the 'body' were a figment of Voss' and Mant's imaginations. Yet another provided full props, including a full-length dummy!

It is entirely up to you how you decide to proceed.

The play should last between 15–20 minutes and will, therefore, give you sufficient time on stage to have your work evaluated. If you have less time, or feel 20 minutes is too long, the second scene could, theoretically, be performed on its own.

Finally, you are encouraged to go and see, or read, two other plays which influenced this one: *Waiting for Godot* by Samuel Beckett and *The Dumb Waiter* by Harold Pinter.

Watching Brief
by Mike Gould

Characters:
- Voice
- Voss
- Mant
- Juno
- Penn

Scene 1 (*A room with a single chair in the middle*)

Voice: Tell us about yourself.

Voss: You know it all already.

Voice: Indulge us.

Voss: What can I say? I know things. Know how things work. You don't pull the wool over my eyes. If this were a job interview, you'd be impressed. I could trot out a CV which would… well, suffice to say, no one's ever been disappointed.

I have my standards. Like a job done properly. Not like so many nowadays. Have you noticed how many envelopes are badly sealed? The bit you lick is all crooked, like someone's been in a hurry to stick the flap down. Then there's spoons. I was in a caff the other day, eating an ice-cream, when I noticed the spoon – one of them long ones – was dirty. I called the waitress over. "This spoon is dirty," I said. "No it's not," she said. "It's stained." She handed it back. I ask you.

Voice: Are you up-to-the-minute?

Voss: Very. I'm not one of these people with their head in the sands vis-à-vis IT and all that. No, I invested in my own personal system – all singing, all dancing affair. 'Course, I don't need it. But it pays to keep in touch. What I don't know about PCs you could put on the back of a microchip. No, I believe in communication. Communication with discipline.

(Beat)

I live alone.

Voice: Thank you. That's all.

Voss: Is that it? No cross-examination? No hard guy soft guy?

Voice: None of that.

1 2 3 4 5 6 7 8 9 10

Voss: It's just there's so much more to say. I don't feel I've done myself justice - there's much more to me than meets the eye. So I've been told.

(No response)

Right. I'll see myself out then.

(Blackout. Slowly fade up lights)

Mant: Err. Should I sit down?

Voice: You are sitting down.

(Mant stands up)

Mant: Sorry.

Voice: Sit down.

Mant: Yes. Of course. Sorry.

Voice: Get on with it.

Mant: Right. Well, not much to tell really. I like a good cup of tea – not now of course – unless…? No, sorry… silly thought. Where was I? Yes. Not much to say. Not that I don't have thoughts. No, I have hundreds of the little blighters, milling around like little ants. But without the organisation. I can't… slot them into place. They drive me mad. Milling and milling. I wish I could swot them. But I can't get at them.

Voice: What are these thoughts about?

Mant: You know. Usual things. Football. Shopping. Traffic. Rain. How many bank holidays there are in the year. Do I need an extra layer today. Tea. The usual. But the funny thing is if I ever want to deal with these things, if I ever try to take control… they slither out of my grasp. Like fish. One moment they're milling… like ants, the next they're slithering… like fish. It's most confusing.

Voice: Do you have an attitude?

Mant: I try to. I had one once but it was a bit nasty, so I steered clear for a while. But recently I've tried them again, and I've been pleasantly surprised. I even bought a paper last week. Didn't read it. But it was a start. I get confused by all those faces and celebrities. I don't know who they are. And one week they look happy, the next week they look sad. Makes no sense to me.

Voice: Would you like to be a celebrity?

Mant: Who wouldn't?

(Beat)

Actually, I wouldn't. You're not going to make me a…

Voice: No.

Mant: That's a relief. Couldn't bear more thoughts milling.

Can I go? *(Starts to leave)*

Voice: You already have.

(Mant has disappeared)

Voice: Welcome.

(Penn and Juno emerge into the light from different sides of the acting space)

Penn: You're seeing us together?

Voice: Why not?

Juno: Isn't it a little unnatural?

Voice: I don't think so.

Penn: Well, we're here. We found the place without a problem, didn't we?

Juno: Without a problem. Apart from the parking. The parking was altogether unsatisfactory. Clearly, the system had broken down. The reserved places were taken by cars without stickers.

Penn: And there was a scooter in one space.

Juno: The machine had no change. We had to leave a message.

Voice: You should have thought about change.

Penn: We're used to plastic. When I was a child my mother told me to wash my hands after touching money. You never know where it's been. I have avoided money ever since. Banks and cashpoints don't provide washbasins.

Juno: We are here on time, in any case.

Voice: Yes. I'm impressed.

Juno: It would be easy to be late. Life is full of choices. Lateness is not an accident. I personally always leave myself an extra two hours. Sometimes it means I have time to kill at my rendezvous.

Voice: What do you do?

Juno: I pace up and down. Look at the patterns on the ceiling.

Voice: What if there are no patterns?

Penn: There are always patterns.

Juno: Sometimes there are no ceilings.

(Beat)

Penn: We'd like to say thanks. For the opportunity. It's so good to have a job to do. So… clean. It starts… and it ends. You've done it… or you haven't. So many people miss that chance. The chance to say, "On this day, I did this… "

Juno: Jobs mean a lot. Take away the job, we'd be… unsatisfied.

Penn: Dissatisfied.

Juno: Whatever.

Penn: Whichever.

(Beat)

Juno: Whichever.

Penn: We're lucky to have each other. No need to think about trivial personal details, there's always a blob of humanity intruding in your space. It's a good feeling. We're good for each other.

Juno: Work well as a team.

Voice: How come you arrived through different doors?

Penn: We haven't solved that yet. But be assured we will. There's always an answer where inconsistencies like that are concerned.

Voice: If you say so.

Juno: Should we go now?

Voice: Yes. Do you need change?

Juno: Change?

Voice: Money.

Penn: No – we'll sort it out ourselves. If we're clamped… so be it. Clamping is a necessary evil. Whenever I see those big yellow irons, I think… it's good to know someone's in charge.

Juno: We sometimes say to each other that we wish God…

Voice: Go on…

Juno: … was a traffic-warden.

Penn: Yes. Black uniform. Hand full of stickers and forms. Patrolling everywhere.

Juno: Wouldn't that be a relief?

Voice: Have some money anyway. Here's a ten-pound note.

(Juno and Penn look around, expectantly, until suddenly a note floats down. Juno grabs it, but Penn wrestles it out of her hands, then the two of them pull and wrestle more forcefully until both end up on the floor struggling. Finally with a burst of action the two fall apart, and the note showers in the air like confetti.

Juno and Penn look at each other, embarrassed for a moment or two, and then shamefacedly start picking up the pieces)

Voice: I suggest you go.

Juno: Yes. Right away.

Penn: You can rely on us.

(They exit still picking up small scraps of the note)

Voice: Goodbye.

Scene 2

(A coffin lies on a table. Two men are sitting in chairs nearby. They are drinking tea. Both are wearing long winter coats. They are Mant and Voss)

Mant: Is the tea okay?

Voss: It's fine.

Mant: Not too much sugar?

Voss: No.

Mant: I expect you'd like some more milk…

Voss: No. There's plenty of milk.

Mant: Is it too weak?

Voss: It's fine. Perfect…

Mant: You would say, wouldn't you?

Voss: Of course I would. Why should I lie?

Mant: People do

Voss: Not me.

(Mant gets up: looks at coffin)

Mant: She looks like she could do with a nice cuppa.

Mant: Bit late for that now.

Mant: I'm just saying. A cup of tea perks you up.

Voss: Not when you're dead.

Mant: No. Of course.

Voss: Anyway, she didn't drink tea.

Mant: Didn't drink tea? That's unbelievable! Everyone drinks tea.

Voss: She didn't. They told me.

Mant: Perhaps if she'd had a nice cuppa everyday she'd still be alive…

Voss: I doubt it.

Mant: I wonder what she drank.

Voss: Lucozade apparently. That's what they told me. Bottles of the stuff.

Mant: Lucozade? That's meant to give you strength.

Voss: It's only a drink. Life is more than what you drink. Death is more than what you drink.

Mant: I suppose so. This tea's cold now. Do you think we could have another cup?

Voss: Out of the question.

Mant: Yes, you're right. We don't want to abuse their hospitality.

Voss: Just sit down. Relax.

Mant: *(Sits down)* I wish I'd brought something to read. A comic – or a good novel.

Voss: You should have thought about that. No planning, that's your problem.

Mant: You haven't brought one.

Voss: I don't like reading. I like sitting here. Just thinking.

Mant: What if someone comes?

Voss: We'll cross that bridge when we come to it. There's no law against thinking.

Mant: Still, I wish I had a book.

Voss: Stop going on about books. Never satisfied, that's you. Can't you just enjoy sitting here?

Mant: With her there?

Voss: She can't hurt you.

Mant: It doesn't seem right – enjoying myself – while she's lying there.

Voss: She's got nothing to do with it. You'd be miserable even if she sat up and started knitting.

Mant: That's not fair.

Voss: It's true.

(There's a knock at the door: Voss looks startled, Mant jumps up)

Mant: Who can that be?

Voss: No idea. Quick, throw your coat over the box.

Mant: I'll be cold.

Voss: This is a time for sacrifices. *(Mant does as he's told)* Answer the door. And smile.

(Mant answers the door. In come two women, Penn and Juno, smartly-dressed)

Penn: We got the message.

Mant: What message?

Juno The message asking us to come and help.

Voss: We don't need any help. We're fine.

Penn: Where did the tea come from?

Voss: It was left here. On a brass tray. Just two cups. So you see, no one sent for you.

Juno: The message was quite clear.

Mant: Perhaps they thought we might be getting depressed, looking after…

Voss: *(Interrupts)* Be quiet.

Juno: Looking after what?

Voss He's mad. Doesn't know what he's saying.

Penn: Just as well we came then. Someone needs to take charge. Aren't you gentlemen going to offer us a seat?

Voss: Have these seats.

Juno: No thanks. We'd rather stand.

Penn: There's something fishy going on here. I can tell. There's a smell of something rotten in the air...

Mant: That'd be… *(Realises his mistake, shuts up)*

Penn: What would it be?

Mant: Nothing. Sometimes places have a sort of smell – for no reason.

Juno: Like the smell of fear. *(To Voss)* Don't you agree?

Voss: I hadn't ever considered it.

Juno: Consider it now.

Voss: Well, it's possible.

Juno: But what do you think?

Voss: Yes. The smell of fear is a distinct possibility.

Juno: Well, that's cleared that one up. Glad we agree on something. Now, let's get down to business.

Penn: The fact is, we're here whether you like it or not. And we're not suddenly going to go away...

Mant: Why not? All you need to do is walk over to the door and leave...

Penn: Don't be ridiculous. Are you throwing us out?

Mant: No, of course not... didn't mean to be rude... you're very welcome... it's just...

Juno: What?

Voss: What he's trying to say is that everything's under control.

Juno: You can't just disinvent what's happened. You can't brush us under the carpet.

Mant: There isn't a carpet.

Penn: It's a metaphor. *(To Voss)* He seems a little slow.

Voss: He's always been like that. He'll never change. If it was up to me I'd be delighted for you to stay.

Penn: You seem reasonable. I could do business with you.

Voss: Don't worry, he's harmless. Just ignore his ramblings.

Juno: *(Suddenly noticing the coat draped over the coffin)* Whose is this coat?

Mant: It's mine.

Juno: You must be cold. You're shivering. Why don't you put the coat on?

Mant: I prefer the cold. Some people like extreme heat – that's why they go on package holidays.

Juno: Good point. But, if you prefer the cold – why have you got a coat at all?

Mant: I'm glad you asked me that question.

Penn: Well?

Mant: Well what?

Penn: If you're glad she asked you – what's the answer?

Mant: Do you know, I've clean forgotten the question! My mind is a sieve. One moment words are pouring in, like cabbage water, the next they're rushing out, down the plughole.

Penn: Sit down. *(Mant sits down)* Listen carefully.

Mant: I will.

Penn: If you prefer the cold why have you got a coat?

Mant: Err… well… because…

Voss: It's for me.

Juno: What?

Voss: It's for me – in case I get cold.

Juno: You've got a coat already.

Voss: Ah, yes, but I'm one of those people who love extreme heat. I'm a sucker for package holidays – Benidorm, Marbella, Tenerife, Alcatraz…

Juno: Alcatraz?

Voss: *(Pause)* Alicante.

Juno: You said 'Alcatraz'.

Voss: I meant Alicante. Anyway, the point is I take several a year. I once took ten in six months…

Juno: Fair enough. Looks like everything is in order. How long have you got left?

Mant: They didn't say. I was hoping for another cup of tea.

Juno: That would be abusing their hospitality.

Voss: He knows that.

Penn: You shouldn't take advantage of people.

Voss: Look, I'm sorry to bother you – but we have work to do.

Juno: You should have said.

Mant: It's not much – but it has to be done.

Juno: Don't let us stop you. Go ahead.

Voss: Right. Kneel down Mant.

Mant: Oh yes. I'd forgotten that bit.

(They both kneel. Penn and Juno look on)

Voss: Our Father, which art in heaven, hallowed be thy name…

(He stops, looks up)

Look, I can't do this with you watching…

Penn: Don't mind us.

Voss: Our Father, which art in heaven, hallow…

(He breaks off)

I'm sorry, you'll have to go…

Penn: That's impossible. We're in this together. Of course, you could buy us off…

Voss: What?

Juno: Pay us.

Voss: Pay you? How much?

Juno: Ten pounds.

Penn: Two five pound notes would be better.

Mant: We haven't got that sort of money.

Voss: We're sorry.

Penn: No matter. What about Sellotape?

Voss: We really must get on.

Juno: Have you any Sellotape?

Voss: *(Exasperated)* No! We're right out of Sellotape! This is a Sellotape-free zone. Look, have a heart. Can't you see…

Mant: … we're busy.

Juno: No Sellotape?

Voss: No!

Penn: In that case we'll have to stay.

Voss: All right. If you must. But I can't do this unless the atmosphere's right. Would you turn the lights down?
(Fade lights so that only Voss and Mant are lit by small pool of light)
Close your eyes Mant. Together this time. Remember, we have to do this every half-an-hour or else there'll be questions.

Mant/Voss: Our Father, which art in heaven, hallowed be thy name…

Voss: This in no good. I can feel you watching us.

(Voss looks up)

Voss: They've left!

Mant: That was a close one.

(Both men stand up, relieved)

Wait a moment. My coat… it's gone! The dirty thieving rotten… *(He peers into the coffin)* Voss, come here!

Voss: What's the matter?

Mant: The body! It's gone too! What are we going to do?

Voss: Nothing. What can we do? We'll just have to face the music.

(They slump into their chairs)

Mant: I wish I had a cup of tea…

Voss: No chance of that now. We've blown it.

Mant: Sorry.

Voss: It's not your fault. No one's to blame.

(There are two slow knocks at the door)

Voss: It's them. Let me do the talking

BLACKOUT

Assignments

The following pages provide a number of assignments which you can work through. Some of them involve work with at least one other group member, but all of them involve some writing which is designed to make you think hard about the issues and ideas covered in this course.

The assignments are as follows:

Assignment 1: *The Seven Black Stones:* devised work (myth)

Assignment 2: *A View from the Bridge:* character (Arthur Miller)

Assignment 3: *The Tempest:* monologue (William Shakespeare)

Assignment 4: *The Tempest:* dialogue (William Shakespeare)

Assignment 5: *Fairytaleheart:* setting (Philip Ridley)

Assignment 6: *Oedipus the King:* drama form (Sophocles)

These can all be utilised at any stage of the course, but may be particularly helpful towards the end of your studies, or when your group are looking to develop a longer piece of work.

Writing

The writing tasks suggested will be very good practice in getting you to reflect carefully either about the texts themselves, or your developmental work.

Assignment 1: *The Seven Black Stones*: devised work (myth)

The following myth, which comes originally from France, presents many opportunities for language and movement work. There are two obvious speaking parts, Bernez and the beggar, and the possibility of creating others, such as the girl Bernez loves. The story also lends itself to physical theatre – or dance work – through the moving stones that form a strong part of the story.

Once upon a time, in the village of Plouhinec, lived a young stonemason called Bernez. Near the village was an isolated heath. In the middle of the heath stood seven enormous black stones , the largest of which stood six metres high. The villagers were frightened of these stones, as they believed they could be heard whispering in an evil way as people passed by.

Bernez was not scared of the stones and he often walked through them on his search for work. One day, he climbed up and, while cutting a cross in one of the stones, heard his name called.

Below him was a ragged beggar, who mocked Bernez, saying he was too poor to marry the girl of his dreams.

"But, I have a way for you to get great wealth – and it's right here!"

Bernez asked him to explain. The beggar replied,
"Every hundred years, on midsummer's night, things that are still become free, and free moving things are fixed to the spot. However, if you find a four-leaf clover you can remain unchanged, and while the stones walk to the river to drink, you will find a great treasure under the largest stone."

"What do you want with me?" asked Bernez.

"Ah," said the cunning beggar. "You know this place well. I don't. I am sure you can locate a four-leaf clover here somewhere, and as it is Midsummer's Day, the treasure will be revealed, and we can share it."

Bernez didn't really believe the story, but he felt sorry for the beggar, and as he had nothing better to do, he agreed to look for the rare clover.

By nightfall, he had found a four-leaf clover for himself, and one for the beggar, but was on the point of going home, when, to his amazement the stones began to move as midnight fell! Everything around him froze – birds in mid-air, the swaying grass, all living creatures.

As the stones moved in enormous, slow steps towards the river, Bernez noticed that, sure enough, there was a hoard of glittering treasure in the hole the largest stone had left. The beggar leaped down and handed the treasure up to Bernez, who thrust it into the waiting sacks they had prepared.

Suddenly, the beggar shouted that the stones were returning. Turning to look, Bernez was defenceless as the beggar knocked the clover from his hand.

He laughed wickedly. "You fool! I made a deal with the stones, promising them human blood in return for the treasure."

At that moment the largest stone towered over Bernez ready to crush him, but as he awaited its mighty force he saw the cross he had carved in it glint in the evening moonlight. The beggar cried out angrily at the stone to kill Bernez, but it didn't move. In a fury he beat his fists against it, and in his temper, dropped the clover from his hand. The beggar was instantly turned to stone, and then fell backwards into the hole.

The largest stone moved once again and, avoiding Bernez, crushed the beggar deep into the pit.

Midnight passed, and suddenly the birds started moving, and normality returned. Scarcely able to believe what had happened Bernez looked around. Everything was as it was before, except for the sacks of treasure, lying at his feet.

A wealthy, and wiser man, he returned to his village, and was able to marry his true love.

Writing

There are three points in time when doing this work when you should make notes:

1. After you have read the story, considering opportunities and possibilities on your own.
2. At an early stage in the development process, noting down your group's decisions, the negotiations that went on, and the style and form you opted for.
3. When the rehearsal process is nearing an end, noting changes to the original ideas, and what processes you decided on.

Finally write a full report **after** the performance on your own contribution to the work:
- in developing ideas
- in what you actually did in performance
- WHY you performed as you did
- HOW you would describe the key elements of your and others' work.

Assignment 2: *A View from the Bridge*: character (Arthur Miller)

The following script may be used for a number of purposes:

- as a stimulus for your own devised work
- as a 'controlled test' with a maximum number of hours you are allowed for preparation
- as a script for honing performance skills.

A View from the Bridge by Arthur Miller.

The play, *A View from the Bridge*, was first performed in 1956. Written by one of America's foremost playwrights, it tells the story of Eddie, a longshoreman (dockworker) in Brooklyn who, with his wife Beatrice, brings up Catherine, their niece, after her parents' death. They have recently taken in some illegal immigrants, Marco and Rodolpho, ('submarines' as they are called because they were smuggled in the bottom of ships). They have arrived from Italy to find work. Rodolpho and Catherine are beginning to fall in love and, although Eddie objects, he does not admit the real reason for this – his own jealousy and attraction to his niece.

The following extract occurs halfway through Act 1. Rodolpho and Catherine are returning from the cinema. Eddie is waiting in the street for them, talking to two other longshoremen, Louis and Mike.

Louis [*– sits on railing beside **Eddie***]: Believe me, Eddie, you got a lotta credit comin' to you.

Eddie: Aah, they don't bother me, don't cost me nutt'n.

Mike: That older one, boy, he's a regular bull. I seen him the other day liftin' coffee bags over the Matson Line. They leave him alone he woulda load the whole ship by himself.

Eddie: Yeah, he's a strong guy, that guy. Their father was a regular giant, supposed to be.

Louis: Yeah, you could see. He's a regular slave.

Mike [*grinning*]: That blond one, though – [***Eddie** looks at him.*] He's got a sense of humour. [***Louis** snickers.*]

Eddie [*searchingly*]: Yeah. He's funny –

Mike [*starting to laugh*]: Well, he ain't exackly funny, but he's always like makin' remarks like, y'know? He comes around, everybody's laughin'. [***Louis** laughs.*]

Eddie [*uncomfortably grinning*]: Yeah, well... he's got a sense of humour.

Mike [*laughing*]: Yeah, I mean, he's always makin' like remarks, like, y'know?

Eddie: Yeah, I know. But he's a kid yet, y'know? He's – he's just a kid, that's all.

Mike [*getting hysterical with **Louis***]: I know. You take one look at him – everybody's happy. [***Louis** laughs.*] I worked one day with him last week over the Moore-MacCormack Line, I'm tellin' you they was all hysterical. [***Louis** and he explode in laughter.*]

Eddie: Why? What'd he do?

Mike: I don't know... he was just humorous. You never can remember what he says, y'know? But it's the way he says it. I mean he gives you a look sometimes and you start laughin'!

Eddie: Yeah. [*Troubled*] He's got a sense of humour.

Mike [*gasping*]: Yeah.

Louis [*rising*] Well, we see ya, Eddie.

Eddie: Take it easy.

Louis: Yeah. See ya.

Mike: If you wanna come bowlin' later we're goin' Flatbush Avenue. [*Laughing they move to exit, meeting* ***Rodolpho*** *and* ***Catherine*** *entering on the street. Their laugher rises as they see* ***Rodolpho*** *who doesn't understand but joins in.* ***Eddie*** *moves to enter the house as* ***Louis*** *and* ***Mike*** *exit.* ***Catherine*** *stops him at the door*]

Catherine: Hey, Eddie – what a picture we saw! Did we laugh!

Eddie [*he can't help smiling at sight of her*]: Where'd you go?

Catherine: Paramount. It was with those two guys, y'know? That –

Eddie: Brooklyn Paramount?

Catherine [*with an edge of anger, embarrassed before* ***Rodolpho***]: Sure, the Brooklyn Paramount. I told you we wasn't goin' to New York.

Eddie [*retreating before the threat of her anger*]: All right, I only asked you. [*To* ***Rodolpho***] I just don't want her hangin' around Times Square, see? It's full of tramps over there.

Rodolpho: I would like to go to Broadway once, Eddie. I would like to walk with her once where the theatres are and the opera. Since I was a boy I see pictures of those lights.

Eddie [*his little patience waning*]: I want to talk to her a minute, Rodolpho. Go inside, will you?

Rodolpho: Eddie, we only walk together in the streets. She teaches me.

Catherine: You know what he can't get over? That there's no fountains in Brooklyn!

Eddie [*smiling unwillingly*]: Fountains? [***Rodolpho*** *smiles at his own naiveté*]

Catherine: In Italy he says, every town's got fountains, and they meet there. And you know what? They got oranges on the trees where he comes from, and lemons. Imagine – on the trees? I mean it's interesting. But he's crazy for New York.

Rodolpho [*attempting familiarity*]: Eddie, why can't we go once to Broadway – ?

Eddie: Look, I gotta tell her something –

Rodolpho: Maybe you can come too. I want to see all those lights. [*He sees no response in* ***Eddie's*** *face. He glances at* ***Catherine***] I'll walk by the river before I go to sleep. [*He walks off down the street*]

Catherine: Why don't you talk to him, Eddie? He blesses you, and you don't talk to him hardly.

Eddie [*enveloping her with his eyes*]: I bless you and you don't talk to me.

Writing

Choose a character from this scene and write detailed notes on how you would choose to play him or her. Make sure you mention gesture, movement, tone of voice, and the interplay with the other characters. Also, make close reference to the stage directions in brackets and how they help you. Then move into groups, allocate roles and prepare a performance.

Assignment 3: *The Tempest*: monologue (William Shakespeare)

The following is a mini-monologue by Caliban. Here, he is talking to the crew shipwrecked on the island. He describes the features of the island, and also provides a different view of himself as a character within the play — perhaps not so much of a monster.

It can be used for:

- your own personal preparation at speaking monologues
- as a speech that could be added to a shortened version of *The Tempest* to go with the work done in Chapter 10.

Be not afeard; the isle is full of noises,
Sounds and sweet airs, that give delight and hurt not.
Sometimes a thousand twangling instruments
Will hum about mine ears; and sometime voices
That, if I then had waked after long sleep,
Will make me sleep again; and then, in dreaming,
The clouds methought would open, and show riches
Ready to drop on me, that when I waked
I cried to dream again.

Writing

Describe, in your own words, how you visualise Caliban on stage. He has been played as a monster, as a wronged slave, as a joker, even as a poetic dreamer. How would you play him? If necessary, go back and reread the work on Caliban in Chapter 10.

Assignment 4: *The Tempest*: dialogue (William Shakespeare)

In Chapter 10, you looked at a dialogue between Prospero and his slave Caliban – a relationship which had soured since Prospero took over the island. Prospero's other servant is a magical spirit, Ariel. Towards the end of the play, Ariel rounds up some of Prospero's enemies, two comical and drunken sailors, who have been joined by Caliban, and leads them towards their punishment. This extract can be used as a good counterpoint to the earlier one.

Perform the dialogue in pairs. If you wish, work with other members of your group who could enact a 'parallel scene' showing the behaviour of the 'varlets' Ariel has dealt with.

Prospero: Say again, where didst thou leave these varlets?

Ariel: I told you, sir, they were red-hot with drinking,
So full of valour that they smote the air
For breathing in their faces, beat the ground
For kissing of their feet; yet always bending
Towards their project. Then I beat my tabor,
At which, like unbacked colts, they pricked their ears,
Advanced their eyelids, lifted up their noses
As they smelt music. So I charmed their ears
That calf-like they my lowing followed, through
Toothed briars, sharp furzes, pricking goss, and thorns,
Which entered their frail shins. At last I left them
I'th'filthy mantled pool beyond your cell,
There dancing up to th'chins, that the foul lake
O'erstunk their feet.

Prospero: This was well done, my bird!
Thy shape invisible retain thou still.
The trumpery in my house, go bring it hither,
For stale to catch these thieves.

Ariel: I go, I go!

Writing

Ariel's words give yet another view of the island. Contrast this with Caliban's words on page 134. How do you visualise the set for this play? How could you represent all the different features? Consider sound and stage design in particular.

Assignment 5: *Fairytaleheart*: setting (Philip Ridley)

Read the following opening of the play, *Fairytaleheart*.

The stage of an abandoned community centre in the East End of London. Most of the windows are broken and boarded over (concealing the snowy, March evening outside) so what is about to be described is, for the moment, barely discernible.

There's a couple of old chairs, several boxes, a table and various scattered detritus. The table is covered with painting materials: brushes, tubes of paint, spray paint, whatever is needed to have created –

The fairytale backdrop. This covers most of the stage and has been created by adapting and painting found objects: a pile of boxes has become a mountain; an old mantelpiece, a cave; a sheet of corrugated iron, a river; a large mirrorball, a sun or moon. Also depicted are birds, flowers and butterflies.

Some distance from the main backdrop – and lying flat on the ground – is a large mirror. Flowers have been painted round it, giving the impression of a pond.

The general effect is of a magical landscape, somewhere between a painting and sculpture. The magical quality will eventually intensify by the shimmering light of –

Candles. These are everywhere on stage: across the floor, on table. Candles of all shapes and sizes. Most are in coloured-glass containers. They are, of course, unlit at present.

Pause.

Then –

The entrance at the back of the auditorium noisily unlocks and –

Kirsty enters. She is fifteen years old and carrying a bag of hastily-packed clothes in one hand and a torch in the other. She is shivering against the cold outside. Hardly surprising considering her clothing – obviously her 'party best': a dress decorated with silver sequins and rhinestones, silver stilettos and a short, white, fake-fur coat. Her hair is neatly styled and highlighted with silver glitter. She's tried hard to make an impression and succeeded.

Kirsty closes the door behind her and switches on the torch. The beam of light pokes through the darkness like a luminous finger.

Kirsty: Hello?

Slight pause.

Kirsty: Anyone there?

Writing

Write a comparison of the stage/set description above, with those provided in any other play of your choosing. Comment in particular on the detail given and what atmosphere is intended by the writers.

Assignment 6: *Oedipus the King*: drama form (Sophocles, translated by David Glene)

In this extract, Oedipus is trying to find out the truth of his own birth and wants to question the shepherd who was responsible for saving his life when he was abandoned in the desert. However, his wife Jocasta realises that Oedipus is none other than her son and that when the shepherd appears the truth of how she tried to kill her own son will come out.

In groups of 4–5 perform the scene several times.

Oedipus: Is he alive
still, so that I could see him?
Messenger: You who live here
would know that best.
Oedipus: Do any of you here
know of this shepherd whom he speaks about
in town or in the fields? Tell me. It's time
that this was found out once for all.
Chorus: I think he is none other than the peasant
whom you have sought to see already;
but Jocasta here can tell us best of that.
Oedipus: Jocasta, do you know about this man
whom we have sent for? Is he the man he mentions?
Jocasta: Why ask of whom he spoke? Don't give it heed;
nor try to keep in mind what has been said.
It will be wasted labour.
Oedipus: With such clues
I could not fail to bring my birth to light.
Jocasta: I beg of you – do not hunt this out – I beg you,
if you have any care for your own life.
What I am suffering is enough.
Oedipus: Keep up
your heart, Jocasta. Though I'm proved a slave,
thrice slave, and though my mother is thrice slave,
you'll not be shown to be of lowly lineage.
Jocasta: O be persuaded by me, I entreat you; do not do this.
Oedipus: I will not be persuaded to let be the chance of finding out
the whole thing clearly.
Jocasta: It is because I wish you well that I give you this counsel – and
it's the best counsel.
Oedipus: Then the best counsel vexes me, and has for some while since.
Jocasta: O Oedipus, God help you!
God keep you from the knowledge of who you are!

Writing

How can this extract be performed without becoming melodramatic? Think about Jocasta's performance in particular. If you need to remind yourself of the whole story, look again at Chapter 9.

Glossary of Terms

Accent	particular sound made in pronouncing words which suggests place or background of speaker
Attack	term used informally to describe strong entrance in speaking
Annotation	(usually) hand-written notes or sketches around a script or other text.
Beat	a pause
Blocking (1)	organisation of movements on the stage
Blocking (2)	unhelpful barrier to development of drama work
Broadway	centre of commercial theatre in New York
Character	usually taken to mean part being played in a drama, or the 'personality' of said part
Chorus	one or more characters who comment on the action
Cliché	over-used phrase ('sick as a parrot') or movement which has lost its original power
Collage	selection of diverse images or pieces of text
Commentary	thoughts about performance or other work
Contrast	difference or opposite
Convention	agreed way of doing things
Dialogue	any speech on stage
Duologue	speech between two characters
Diaphragm	pit of the stomach
Divali	Hindu festival, celebrated around October
Dynamic	relationship between two or more things or people
Element	part
Empathy	sense of being able to 'put yourself in someone else's shoes'
Emphasis	added strength given to word, sound or action
End-on stage	type of stage in which the 'fourth wall' (the others being the sides and back of stage) is created by audience - no proscenium
Entrance	point or place where actor comes in
Evaluation	reflection about success of work
Exit	point or place where actor leaves
Exploration	development of ideas through questioning and trying out possibilities
Focus	attention on specific detail
Form	shape or pattern of the drama
Framing	image created by whole view of stage or a group of actors
Function	role or part
Genre	particular style or set of conventions or forms
Gesture	physical movement
Hot-seating	technique whereby actors are questioned in role about their behaviour
Improvisation	developing drama from initial input, usually without script
Interplay	way two or more characters act and speak together
Interpretation	particular belief and decision about way a text should be performed
Light opera	musical drama often with comic elements
Melodrama	highly-stylised and sentimental drama
Mime	non-speaking movement work
Minimalist	stripped-bare drama (few props or set)
Monologue	single, long speech by one character

Motive	reason for behaviour
Multiple	many
Narrative	story or plot
Naturalistic	imitating real-life
Nativity play	(usually) childlike drama about the birth of Christ, often performed by children
Neologism	made-up word
Perspective	view
Physical	relating to body or movement work
Pace	speed
Pitch	level – high or low, as in music
Plot	story or narrative
Practical	actual work as it happens; contrast to theoretical
Prop	object used on stage
Prose	continuous text; not verse
Process	continual development of work
Proscenium/arch	traditional stage form in which audience view action through 'arch' made in the stage wall.
Rhythm	beat and regular pattern of sounds
Ritual	presentation developed over time of religious or cultural concerns
Sequence	related or repeated set of actions
Sight-lines	view from various angles of stage or actors
Soliloquy	single speech by one character
Source	place from which ideas come (e.g. photo, image, etc.)
Spontaneous	on the spot, without preparation
Stage directions	notes for actors or directors regarding where and when the cast enter, leave etc.
Stance	position taken by an actor on stage
Status	level of power
Story-board	set of drawn images used to describe a story
Stress	emphasis on sounds or words
Style	type or form
Syllable	sound-part of a word
Symbol	object which suggests or represents an idea or set of ideas
Tableau	('frozen tableau') – group of performers creating a frozen statue to represent something
Technique	presented skill
Tempo	pace or speed
Terminology	set of words used to describe something
Thrust stage	stage surrounded on three sides by audience
Tragedy	classically, a story in which a great man or woman is brought down by a fault in their character
Utterance	sound
Verse	lines laid out as poetry; as opposed to prose
Vowel	a, e, i, o, u
Warm-up	preparatory exercise used before main work
West End	centre of commercial theatre in London

Index of Writers and Texts

Oedipus Rex